BECOMING A SUCCESSFUL SCHOOL LEADER

C000127619

Becoming a Successful School Leader critically considers what leaders need to help them support their schools and communities with the challenges and demands of learning. It presents readers with opportunities to develop their thinking and generate personal strategies to manage situations through a series of structured exercises and tasks.

Drawing on a range of accounts from professionals, case studies and reflective questions, this accessible text allows leaders to confidently guide their staff and students through the contested landscape of education. Focusing on key topics, chapters cover:

- education policy and leadership, governance and management of educational settings;
- changes to the employment market;
- inclusion in education, emerging moral dilemmas and legislative changes;
- the structure of education: new frameworks and models;
- quality assurance: responsibilities, liabilities and consequences;
- global dimensions and emerging ethical issues.

This book will be essential reading for both practising and aspiring school leaders who have an interest in the challenges, policies and practices deployed in leading and managing change in a variety of educational settings.

Krishan Sood is Senior Lecturer at Nottingham Trent University, UK. He began his career as a Science teacher in a secondary school, going on to lead a department and become an advisory teacher for intercultural education.

Sheine Peart is Manager of the PhD Education course at Nottingham Trent University, UK. She has worked in education for over 30 years in schools, colleges, local authorities, further education, higher education and youth and community settings.

Malini Mistry is Senior Lecturer in Early Years at the University of Bedfordshire, UK. Although she specialised in Early Years education, she has worked within the whole primary phase, leading and managing many areas of the curriculum.

BECOMING A SUCCESSFUL SCHOOL LEADER

Developing New Insights

Krishan Sood, Sheine Peart and Malini Mistry

LONDON AND NEW YORK

First published 2018
by Routledge
2 Park Square, Milton Park, Abingdon, Oxon OX14 4RN

and by Routledge
711 Third Avenue, New York, NY 10017

Routledge is an imprint of the Taylor & Francis Group, an informa business

© 2018 Krishan Sood, Sheine Peart and Malini Mistry

British Library Cataloguing in Publication Data
A catalogue record for this book is available from the British Library

Library of Congress Cataloging in Publication Data
Names: Sood, Krishan, author. | Peart, Sheine, author. | Mistry, Malini, author.
Title: Becoming a successful school leader : developing new insights / Krishan Sood, Sheine Peart and Malini Mistry.
Description: Abingdon, Oxon ; New York, NY : Routledge, 2018. | Includes index.
Identifiers: LCCN 2017008631| ISBN 9781138100541 (hardback) | ISBN 9781138100558 (pbk.) | ISBN 9781315657615 (ebook)
Subjects: LCSH: Educational leadership—Great Britain. | School management and organization—Great Britain.
Classification: LCC LB2900.5 .S66 2018 | DDC 371.2--dc23
LC record available at https://lccn.loc.gov/2017008631

ISBN: 978-1-138-10054-1 (hbk)
ISBN: 978-1-138-10055-8 (pbk)
ISBN: 978-1-315-65761-5 (ebk)

Typeset in News Gothic
by Saxon Graphics Ltd, Derby

CONTENTS

ACKNOWLEDGEMENTS

We would like to thank our respective families for their unconditional support during the long weekends of writing – thank you for your patience and understanding. We would also like to thank our editors Annamarie Kino, Clare Ashworth and Natalie Larkin at Taylor & Francis for their sharp eye and their constant encouragement and feedback – it was much appreciated.

Finally, but by no means least, to all those teachers, headteachers, support staff, Local Authority staff, student teachers, governors, Kamal, Jo, Lisa, Nicola, Emma, Angela and Anne, who enrich the learner-centred practice – thank you for the ideas you gave us for some of the examples used in this book.

1   Introduction

Leadership for the future

Chapter aims

When you have finished reading this chapter you will be able to:

1. recognise the importance of this text to contemporary education leaders;
2. appreciate the key features of this book and their significance;
3. understand how to use this book for maximum benefit and impact.

Overview of chapter

This book has been written for all staff who work in education as a teacher, trainer, manager or learning support worker based in broad range of different settings, including Early Years, primary, secondary, further education and higher education. In each of these roles in different education settings, all staff, at some stage, will have to make leadership decisions regarding how learning will be managed which will have a direct impact on learners and their learning experience.

   The purpose of this chapter is simply to explain how this book is organised and to give you a map to help you use the book efficiently. Although the authors hope you will want to read the entire book and will find it both useful and informative, it is realistically acknowledged you will probably find some chapters and exercises more relevant than others. Accepting everyone who works in education is extremely busy, with many pressing demands placed on their time, this chapter has been provided to help you decide which chapters you feel are immediately relevant to you and you need to read now, and to help you plan the order you will read the remaining chapters in.

Key words: leadership; learners; learning; organisation.

Introduction

'The dominant understanding of educational equality in contemporary Anglo-American political discourse is meritocratic' (Brighouse et al., 2010: 27); and these 'liberal, democratic, meritocratic ideals' (Wright et al., 2010: 117) demand students' abilities should dictate individual learning outcomes within education. However, sometimes structures, systems and the environment come together to produce learning outcomes which are not solely based on a student's ability. Education leaders need to manage history, contemporary demands and events to make decisions to service the needs of learners so all learners can achieve their potential and enjoy a positive experience of education.

This book has been written to help you understand the broad range of leadership issues and to give you an opportunity to work out the challenges and issues you face in your working life. This book cannot give you an answer to every situation you encounter. However, the detailed case studies and reflective questions and discussions which feature in each chapter will support you to consider your personal responses to different situations, help you to plan how you might manage these issues, support you to develop the skills needed to tackle difficult situations, and signpost you to relevant support agencies.

While some of the chapter case studies and tasks take a sector-specific focus, the skills and awareness developed through task completion are transferable to other settings. Further it is necessary to remember that learners will have moved from one setting to another and it is important for leaders to understand learners' histories so that they can help learners manage their present realities and make plans for their futures.

Structure and organisation of this book

Each chapter in this book is structured in the same way and has the same set of learning features. This is to help you to swiftly become familiar with the book's organisation and make best use of the information provided. All chapters begin with a set of learning aims. These specify the skills, knowledge and understanding you can expect to develop by reading the chapter and by working through the structured exercises provided. Chapter aims are actively expressed and identify what you will be able to do after reading the chapter. A chapter overview provides detail of the theory covered and gives information about some of the issues and challenges faced by contemporary leaders. The overview provides a synopsis of the chapter and will allow you to decide if reading this chapter is a priority for you. A short list of key words follows the overview and identifies a maximum of six key terms covered in the chapter and supports further literature searches readers may wish to undertake.

In the body of the text, each chapter starts with a short introduction which outlines the main issues covered. The chapter is then subdivided by a series of sub-headings which describe a particular subject, issue or problem supported by the relevant academic literature and theory. Where relevant, tables have been used to either summarise or organise data. Each chapter has a series of case studies, reflective questions and discussions. These are key activities designed to develop your skill set. Case studies are used to illustrate a scenario or event. Each case study is based on a real-life situation and describes actual events. After each case study and in other places in the chapter, reflective questions ask you to consider how you would respond to a particular situation. When responding to the reflective questions, you should reflect on your personal experiences and use the theory provided to help you formulate your answer. The questions are designed to provoke and challenge your thinking and enable you to develop new responses. Although some of the situations provided may not appear immediately relevant to you in your current circumstances, working through the questions will help you to decide on action should you encounter a similar situation. Discussions which follow reflective questions draw together theory and practice to suggest an appropriate leadership response. While the discussions identify a suitable way forward, it is important to remember all responses need to be contextualised and what may be suitable in one situation may not be acceptable in another environment. However, while leaders may make an appropriate localised response, all leaders are obliged to ensure their actions are legislatively compliant.

Each chapter ends with a summary which draws together the main points of the chapter, followed by a reference list of all texts and literature used.

Chapter summaries

Chapter 2 begins by reviewing policy, leadership, governance and management issues for education settings. It considers policy formation and the range of different policy initiatives generated by central government which education leaders are obliged to implement. It reviews the challenges of implementing these different policies in difficult circumstances. The case studies and reflective questions ask readers to critically examine policy implementation in their own settings, to identify local challenges and to explain how these were managed.

Chapter 3 considers one of the major challenges faced by all education leaders: recruiting and maintaining an appropriate staffing team to meet the needs of learners. Using a structural framework for managing education environments developed by the National College for Teaching and Leadership, the chapter explores issues of recruitment, managing staffing shortages and the range of staff contracts available. It reviews the specific obligations placed on leaders when employing international staff and how this particular solution may also create a range of issues which leaders would need to resolve. It reviews the ethical dilemmas leaders need to work through when trying to ensure they have a full, appropriately qualified staff team to drive their organisation forward.

Education is bound by statute. Education leaders must ensure they fully comply with all relevant legislation and cannot choose which parts of legislation they will implement. The 2010 Equality Act and 2015 statutory Code of Practice on Special Educational Needs and Disability reinforced equality legislation and introduced new requirements for education settings. Chapter 4 explores how equality legislation actively supports learners and learning and how ethical working practices support learner achievement. The chapter explores the need for strong, morally driven leadership to enable education settings to accelerate and achieve positive change.

Beginning with a brief historical overview, reflecting a time when local authorities directly controlled schools and their budgets, Chapter 5 examines how successive governments (Conservative, Labour and Coalition alike) have worked to limit centralisation while increasing organisational accountability through various government agencies including Ofsted. The chapter considers how traditional settings such as local authority schools now share the educational landscape with other, newer types of organisation including academies and free schools. As central control and support has reduced, education settings have needed to consider other options to provide essential services. The chapter reviews the new multi-agency partnerships education leaders have had to explore and establish to meet the needs of their learning communities.

Quality and quality assurance are an essential part of education leadership. Leaders need to be confident that learners are benefiting from the best education possible and their staffing teams are providing the highest quality learning experiences. Robust quality-assurance procedures are the mechanism which enable leaders to have this confidence. Chapter 6 reviews how leaders can manage the demands placed on them in implementing quality assurance systems which are both understood and owned by staff teams together with an examination of the boundaries of accountability and responsibility. It considers the tension of how such accountability can be motivational to some staff who may want to achieve new goals while other staff may find such scrutiny threatening and demotivating.

Chapter 7 considers the implications of service-user voice and how education organisations need to positively respond to a much broader range of users including parents, carers and learners themselves. The chapter considers the skill set needed by staff to accurately capture the range of user views and useful structures to establish to support this process. Case studies and reflective questions support readers to critically examine practice in their settings, to recognise areas of best practice and identify areas of improvement.

There is a developing dilemma in education as fewer and fewer staff elect to take on leadership roles. Chapter 8 examines how this issue can be addressed and what preparation is needed to enable new leaders to fully embrace the challenges and responsibilities of leading in education. The chapter considers succession planning and how organisations can work to ensure there is a constant supply of aspirant leaders ready to assume responsibility within the organisation as others leave, for example to take on roles in different settings.

Education settings are not islands. They are connected to and are part of wider networks. With growing technological capability, the level of interconnectivity and mutual reliance has increased and education settings are now part of global education communities. While operating on a world stage confers many advantages, it also produces significant challenges.

Using primary education as a case setting and critical race theory as a lens for examination, Chapter 9 explores some of the issues raised by globalisation, what it means to education settings and how leaders can work to develop ethical global practices in their settings for the benefit of all learners.

Chapter 10 discusses the changing role of leaders in Early Years settings. It considers the rapid changes these leaders have had to manage in response to the Early Years Foundation Stage (EYFS) Statutory Framework supported by the Department for Education (DfE) and scrutinised by Ofsted.

Chapter 11 draws together the key messages from the book, reviews the implications for leaders in different sectors and suggests positive ways forward for leadership within education organisations.

Summary

Education is a vast, heterogeneous community populated by learners of all abilities serviced by an increasingly diverse staff. This book examines the responsibilities of education leaders in meeting the needs of learners in all sectors by working with and through their staff teams to achieve educational excellence.

Education leaders are charged with the weighty responsibility of leading their organisations in a constantly changing turbulent environment. They are ultimately responsible for all of the organisation's achievements but as the adage reminds us, while 'success has many parents' and countless people will want to share such success, when an organisation fails the leader alone is held accountable. This book provides theoretical frameworks and practical suggestions to support leaders to meet structural, academic and other challenges. It is for those leaders 'who are willing to try new approaches and who want to be part of a change to promote … educational achievement' (Peart, 2013: 5) for all their learners and the communities they serve.

References

Brighouse, H., Tooley, J. and Howe, K. R. (2010) *Educational Equality.* London: Continuum.

Peart, S. (2013) *Making Education Work: How Black Men and Boys Navigate the Further Education Sector.* London: Trentham, Institute of Education Press.

Wright, C., Standen, P. and Patel, T. (2010) *Black Youth Matters.* Abingdon: Routledge.

2 Education policy and leadership, governance and management of educational settings

Chapter aims

When you have finished reading this chapter you will be able to:

1. identify the different types of educational settings in England;
2. know how education policy is formed and how leaders implement it in different sectors of education;
3. understand and explain what the drivers are in developing education policy;
4. be aware of the role of leadership and governors in addressing the impact of education policy in different school types.

Overview of chapter

This chapter develops your understanding about how education policy is influenced and formed by different external and internal factors, known as drivers. Different types of educational settings will use different strategies to develop policies related to their specific context reflecting global and local trends, called megatrends (explained later). Any education policy implemented from a national (macro level) to local school (micro level) is reliant on leadership at all levels of the system. Here, the system is the school. Currently, there is a move for leadership to be practised holistically and system-wide, which means that every member of staff has a role in leading educational provision at classroom (meso level). This is called systemic leadership in action. Leadership in education is about all staff and governors offering a clear route map (policy) to improve educational outcomes for learners (Bell and Stevenson, 2006).

Introduction

The world of education is changing rapidly, and with it, a new world is emerging for leaders, practitioners and school governance. We look at some of the changes, challenges and opportunities this world of school governance brings. We pose the questions of where we are now and where we should be going, as well as what do we know and what do we need to know. With the educational landscape showing an increasing number of schools becoming 'independent' as academies or free schools, and with the ever decreasing role and capacity of Local Authorities (LAs), school governing boards are having to be held accountable for continuing effectiveness and probity of schools with little help or advice from LAs. This chapter will look at exploring issues of policy and practice from a number of perspectives and for readers themselves to challenge and refine their own views.

Key words: collegiality; different school types; governance; leadership.

Different types of education system in England

Let us briefly look at an overview of the education system in England. All learners in England between the ages of 5 and 16 are entitled to a free place at a state school, and this is compulsory. The most common schools are:

Table 2.1 Different types of schools in England

School type	Function
Community schools	Controlled by the local council and not influenced by business or religious groups.
Foundation schools	Have more freedom to change the way they develop their policies and actions than community schools.
Academies	Run by a governing body, independent from the local council – they can follow a different curriculum.
Grammar schools	Run by the council, a foundation body or a trust – they select all or most of their learners based on academic ability and there is often an exam to get in.
Special schools	For learners aged 11 and older. They can specialise in one of the four areas of special educational needs: • cognition and learning; • social, emotional and mental health; • sensory and physical needs. Schools can further specialise within these categories to reflect the special needs they help with, for example autistic spectrum disorders, visual impairment or speech, language and communication needs (SLCN) (gov.uk, 2016: online).
Free schools	Can set their own pay and conditions for staff and change the length of school terms and the school day. They do not have to follow the National Curriculum. Free schools are run on a not-for-profit basis and can be set up by groups like charities, universities, independent schools, community and faith groups, teachers, parents and businesses.
University technical colleges	These specialise in subjects like engineering and construction – and teach these subjects along with business skills and using IT. Learners study academic subjects as well as practical subjects leading to technical qualifications. The university and the employers who provide work experience for learners design the curriculum. Universities, employers and further education colleges sponsor university technical colleges.

Table 2.1 continued

School type	Function
Studio schools	These are small schools – usually with around 300 learners – delivering mainstream qualifications through project-based learning. This means working in realistic situations as well as learning academic subjects. Learners work with local employers and a personal coach, and follow a curriculum designed to give them the skills and qualifications they need in work, or to take up further education.
Faith schools	These schools can be different kinds of schools, for example voluntary aided schools, free schools, academies etc., but are associated with a particular religion. Faith schools are mostly run like other state schools. They have to follow the National Curriculum except for religious studies, where they are free to only teach about their own religion. The admissions criteria and staffing policies may be different too, although anyone can apply for a place.
City technology colleges	City technology colleges are independent schools in urban areas that are free to attend. They are owned and funded by companies as well as central government (not the local council). They have a particular emphasis on technological and practical skills.
State boarding schools	State boarding schools provide free education but charge fees for boarding. Local councils run some state boarding schools, and some are run as academies or free schools. State boarding schools give priority to learners who have a particular need to board and will assess learners' suitability for boarding.
Private schools	Private schools (also known as 'independent schools') charge fees to attend instead of being funded by the government. Learners do not have to follow the National Curriculum. All private schools must be registered with the government and are inspected regularly.

You can see that with such an array of schools in England, the strategy, policy and planning management becomes quite a challenge for leaders and governors. We develop the implications for developing policy in these settings later in this chapter.

 Activity: Challenges of working in different settings

The types of school shown in Table 2.1 pose many challenges and opportunities concerning what works, what does not and why. For example, take partnership working with other settings. What are some of the challenges of setting up meetings? How will you overcome challenges like communicating the agenda to all, organising and agreeing dates to meet, getting all/most people to attend, etc.? If there were not a quota of people to meet, what would you do next? Please identify your own setting and consider what these challenges/opportunities are for you.

Through reflecting on this activity with different colleagues, you will have a better idea about what works in such different settings. In the scenario offered above regarding arranging partnership meetings, you will note how frustrating it is to get everyone together, and this takes up much valuable time, energy and sometimes only helps to raise the blood pressure! For example, how do you develop a marking policy or recruitment policy or equal opportunities policy in a state school? Here, what may work well is understanding that the role of governors in developing school policies is becoming more prominent under the guise of accountability. Therefore, the first step is to develop a working partnership with all relevant parties, so that all voices are represented in policy development. After all, an agreed consensus view is more likely to reap end rewards. You will note that as the policy develops, you debate the issues, exchange ideas, share values and beliefs more openly, and this minimises any tensions.

How education policy is formed – changes, challenges and opportunities of managing megatrends

Policy development

A policy is a statement of intent. It signifies how an organisation is going to be led. This requires the development of 'clear principles for managing and the anticipation of a medium-to long term view of desired outcomes' (West-Burnham, 1994: 79). Strategy is therefore required for effective management for effective outcomes in learning, resource management, and staff deployment and its monitoring and evaluation of success. Caldwell and Spinks (1988) suggest that effective policy development requires the involvement of people in change management by offering feedback to the leadership team on what works and what does not, and is therefore a continuous process. Marsh (1993) reinforces the idea of a strategic planning process and states that at the heart of planning and strategy lies the central focus on students, whom he calls customers. He goes on to say that any process of planning is not without its problems, such as ensuring the timing is right or there are adequate resources available for change management. This therefore requires strong leadership from the head and the governors to translate vision into purposeful practice (Armstrong, 2009).

Managing megatrends – changes, challenges and opportunities

Leaders, governors and staff face multiple changes and the challenges of new educational landscape such as a changing curriculum within different contexts. It is new and challenging to lead and manage the different educational settings in existence now such as trusts, academies, faith schools, independent and state schools, both comprehensive and grammar, as described earlier. These trends, or rather *megatrends*, are so called because they are the 'big issues' of current educational times, and they have to be led and managed sensitively.

To manage megatrends requires an understanding of policy and strategy implementation. Before we describe these, we explain the various megatrends affecting the education sector and then turn to the characteristics or drivers necessary for schools to manage these trends.

Megatrends

These are a few examples of megatrends:

- international developments;
- globalisation;
- quantum thinking;
- marketing – exchange of value/stakeholder voice.

International developments

We are seeing greater interest in improving education in the UK from looking at international studies. In England, we are fortunate to have many good schools, with good buildings, adequate resources and well-resourced staff. In contrast, in many countries in Africa we find headteachers managing schools with poor buildings, little or no equipment, untrained teachers, lack of basic facilities such as water, power and sanitation, and learners who are often hungry (Bush and Oduro, 2006). What we have learned from international research is that education holds the key to becoming, and remaining, competitive (Hallinger, 2001; Wylie and Mitchell, 2003) and leaders are under pressure to manage increasing complexity and continuous change brought about by this megatrend.

Globalisation

Education is a global interest and concern. With greater mobility, opening up international borders, seeing greater intercommunication globally, we are witnessing the rise of globalisation and greater cultural awareness (Mistry and Sood, 2012). We therefore have to develop technologies to reach out globally with demographic changes (Crow, 2006). This megatrend needs to be managed effectively by leaders developing a global culture in educational contexts through teaching and learning about technological globalisation, economic globalisation, demographic globalisation and political globalisation (Bottery, 2008: 5).

Quantum thinking

Another megatrend to be aware of is quantum thinking. This is the ability of the mind to function at a higher level of creativity and innovation (Innovations International, 2016). It involves a shift from linear thinking to higher-order holistic thinking achieved through the critical skill of personal mastery (Senge, 1990) and positive psychology – for example, a challenge for which there is no ready-made technical answer.

Marketing

Marketing as megatrend is about exchange of value through transaction. However, value implies a perception of benefit or not. For example, a parent acquires information about the school policy from the headteacher or bursar. The bursar gets information about the parent to attract them to the school. Here, bartering appears to happen. There is social value exchange involving some combination of information and affirming relationship. Marketing is a major trend to attract customers or new learners into schools. Therefore, this activity has major impact by which the marketing policy is developed and implemented to attract and retain learners. It requires good understanding of marketisation principles like global influences, managing external relations, accountability, responsiveness, cultural change and managing competitive environment (Foskett, 2002).

Let us look deeper into some of the drivers of education policy.

Drivers of education policy – where are we now and where should we be going?

The characteristics of our current school system – where are we now?

We need to understand the current situation in education in England before we look at the challenges schools face in achieving high standards for all. Given the different types of school settings we currently have here, variation becomes the most fundamental challenge for our education system today. Munby (2012) thinks that while some of our learners are receiving a world-beating standard of education, others are being let down. Not only is there variation in quality of education between schools, but most significantly we can see variation between classrooms within the same school. This could mean that our deprived learners may be receiving the worst deal. We need a level playing field (Wilkinson and Pickett, 2010) where the success of our education system depends on addressing variation.

Munby (2012) suggests that with increased autonomy comes a risk of greater isolationism, with schools failing to share expertise or high-quality practice. Further, diversity can create a barrier that prevents schools from sharing practice and expertise. For example, the main reason for schools not working together to deliver Continuous Professional Development (CPD) is that they perceive other schools to be 'too different' (National College Annual Survey, 2010/11).

Increasingly diverse educational settings in England

Currently, there are approximately 21,000 schools in England, including academies, faith schools, free schools, grammar schools and comprehensive schools. There are 7,318 schools with fewer than 200 pupils and 2,499 with fewer than 100 (Munby, 2012). With such diverse school settings, there is potential for whole-school or system-wide learning from each other. Research from the US Charter Schools (National College

Annual Survey, 2010/11) suggests charter schools offer benefit by creating a competitive pressure on other public schools and so help raise standards. Nevertheless, we need champions in the education sector to develop partnerships and collaborative arrangements to seek maximum advantage from learning from each other. Such change requires strong leadership qualities for changing times – leaders who understand the current ways of working of different educational settings, know how to manage complexity (Grint, 2005) and how to manage adaptive challenge (Heifetz and Linsky, 2002). This adaptive challenge concept means there is no ready-made technical answer available. Therefore, we require change in people's values, beliefs, attitudes and habits of behaviour. This means that policy makers from different educational settings will have to build a coalition within organisations and seek out pragmatic and entrepreneurial solutions. Today's deeply held beliefs about leadership are challenged. Values that made us successful are now less relevant. Skills that made us successful are now less relevant (Heifetz and Linsky, 2002).

Where should we be going?

So going forward, there are many such challenges and opportunities to be explored requiring unconventional solutions. However, there is a danger that we will get more of what we have always had. The new era provides an opportunity to think and act differently. Maybe we have to live with some of our problems as incremental change might be better than failed big bangs – the high jump theory of change (May, 2011).

The essential attributes of policy development mean that an understanding of the interactions between strategic choice, strategic analysis and strategic implementation (Johnson et al., 2008) is necessary. So strategic management requires leaders to undertake a strategic analysis of the environment (external), commercial and political context, and look at opportunities/threats, resources, competencies and capabilities (internal) and the skill sets of people and culture. It requires discussions of expectation and purposes (human influences on strategy), which means analysing stakeholders' influence on culture and therefore strategy.

To travel forward, the policy implementers need to undertake an analysis of the approach to strategy implementation the school will need to adopt, such as:

- Organisation structure and design
  - How we organise
- Resource allocation and control
  - How we do it and are accountable for it
- Managing strategic change
  - How we plan and manage

Moving policy strategy into reality

To move policy strategy into reality requires achieving a mind-shift in creating and sustaining the imperative and taking down the barriers. Here, the most powerful imperative of all is learners' voices. This means policy leaders will have to take the view of different stakeholders such as learners' voices, parents' voices, governors' voices, staff and others requiring participation in current shifting policy and financial climate. Then there have to be monitoring and evaluation systems in place to see if the policies work in reality and to be accountable for actions taken by leadership (Brighouse and Woods, 1999).

 Activity: Strategy

Children were recently asked what kind of schools and education (policy) would they like. They said:

> *Being heard; Good school; Doing well; Parks – safe places to play; Loving families; Help when needed; Being healthy; No bullies; Kind teachers; Being green; Doing things in class; and Drug free*
>
> (Talk presentation by Rachel Dickinson, Strategic Director, Children Leicester City Council, Chair – Leicester Children's Trust, 2012)

So, what do we need to do to improve these children's lives and narrow the gap?

 Discussion: Narrowing the gap

This activity is a much more complex question than it first appears. Assessing common needs, reflecting on each voice and planning a strategy for improvement is what is needed. Policy makers and analysts understand that they need to know what the Indices of Multiple Deprivation (IMD) are for each county. This shows the deprivation experienced based on 38 indicators, grouped under seven domains: income; employment; crime; health deprivation and disability; education, skills and training; barriers to housing and services; living environment. Income and employment carry the heaviest weighting. Then there is complex needs analysis of particular learners and young people who experience multiple disadvantage including:

- disabled learners;
- looked after learners;

- young offenders;
- teenage parents;
- young people who are NEET (Not in Education, Employment or Training);
- children and young people with parents who misuse drugs and alcohol.

Investing in our learners and improving learners' lives is an important vision that will lead to narrowing the gap.

 Reflective questions

Use visual aids (flipchart, IT resource) to show how you might shape the school's provision for all learners. Working in partnership to raise aspiration and build achievement is often cited as a strategy, with the outcomes of raising standards of attainment and closing the well-being gap. Where do you want to be in three years' time?

1. As a team discuss and agree this.
2. Are the right services and responsibilities in the right places in your school?
3. Where do you share responsibilities?
4. Who can help out who in delivering key areas and priorities for your school?
5. What are the barriers for change – what gets in the way?

In reflecting on this activity, you would have concluded the complexity of change management and the need to have a balanced discussion for the best outcome for learners. Defining key roles and responsibilities of individuals is necessary for this activity. Taking an audit of what is available now and where the gaps are is the next step so that strategic implementation of a plan can be actioned. Barriers to change, like time and resources, will have to be resolved as the issues arise. By the end of this process, you will realise that team effort results in positive outcomes, but the individual's role in this activity remains the glue that binds the task with the people.

Policy, change and turbulence – schools as learning organisations

The new world of education is formed of educational trusts, academies, free schools, private and independent schools and state schools. All face changes and challenges and we argue that a learning organisation has apposite capacity to manage turbulence. To survive, organisations must learn at least as fast as the prevalent rate of change. To prosper, they must learn significantly faster than the rate of change. It is worth reflecting on Handy's model of change management for a moment. He noted that everything that is born reaches a peak before the decline. However, organisations have the capacity to 'renew themselves and thereby avoid the inevitable decline' (Handy, 1994: 49). Handy recalls a story of the 'Road to Davy's Bar': 'if you pass Davy's Bar, you've gone too far!!', and from this he draws the conclusion that 'by the time you know where you ought to go, it's too late to go there, or, more dramatically, if you keep on going the way you are, you will miss the road to the future' (Handy, 1994: 49).

Handy introduced the term the Sigmoid curve to explain the many turbulences we face. The curve describes the difficulties of one's life or of a school. To survive the turbulence and grow with confidence and assurance, Handy says we need to start a new Sigmoid curve before the old one begins to recede. As Handy explains:

> The right place to start that second curve is at point A, where there is the time, as well as the resources and the energy, to get the new curve through its initial explorations and flounderings before the first curve begins to dip downwards.
>
> (Handy, 1994: 51)

So not only do we want individual learning but also organisational learning. In individual learning, we go through several stages of learning – doing, reflecting, thinking and deciding (Kolb, 1984). Therefore, individuals may learn using a number of multiple intelligences (Gardner, 1999). To that end, we need to know the nature of knowledge to assess what needs changing for what reason and its impact. Hence the need to gather data, information, so we have detailed knowledge for deeper understanding. In contrast, we also need to be learning organisations where people continually expand their capacity to create the results they truly desire, where new and expansive patterns of thinking are nurtured. Here, collective aspiration is set free and people are continually learning how to learn. The emphasis on individual and organisational learning is deliberate as, individually and

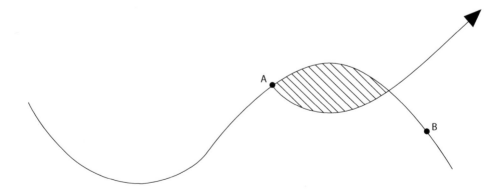

Figure 2.1 The Sigmoid curve (after Handy, 1994: 51)

collectively, people in the different types of schools emerging will have to face such complexities and address these challenges. For example, they will have to look to the future by looking at their present through reflection-in-action, and this may mean learning from each other.

Senge's (1990) learning disciple model offers a helpful guide to change management by developing holistic, system-wide thinking through the four elements: shared vision, mental models, team learning and personal mastery. All may require different organisational learning styles. Maybe the question is not whether your organisation is a learning one, but what kind of organisational learning is going on here. If we see an organisation as a living being, this implies it can evolve naturally, it has its own goals and its own capacity for autonomous action, it can regenerate itself, beyond the current members, people are human communities and it can learn as an entity (De Geus, 1997).

In managing change and turbulence, we consider the following to be the leadership imperatives for the learning organisation:

- Know your team and their level of 'maturity'.
- Know how to select and use appropriate leadership styles.
- Analyse your present structures and processes.
- Scan the external environment to identify the megatrends.
- Be aware of and actively use the processes of individual, team and organisational learning.
- Cultivate an openness to collaborative learning.
- Build synergy through a synthesis of intuitive and rational approaches.
- Use meta-cognition – learn how to learn.
- Develop micro-political skills.

The challenge facing school leaders in different school types described here is that they need to move away from a 'comfortable view of educational leadership related to normative concepts of a heroic or collaborative function' (Lumby, 2015: 2–3). We need further research to understand more about if and how individuals engage with micropolitics in shaping discussion and decisions or weakening oppositions (Samier, 2014) and how this translates into practice on a daily basis.

Leadership and governors' role in addressing the impact of education policy

Earlier, we hinted that educational policy is shaped by ideological foundations often driven by socio-political discourses. The role of governors and leadership of a setting is to help develop a policy taking account of the values of the society based on equality, justice and human rights. These give strategic direction to curriculum formation, access and participation. Policy implementation then follows involving operationalising practices and procedures. In reality, the journey from policy construction to implementation and evaluation for accountability to different stakeholders is thwarted with different challenges and opportunities to shape its construction for the benefits of learners. There are sometimes sharp ideological differences between staff, governors and community, especially concerning culture and ethnicity regarding policy development. Tensions may arise given different power relations when the notion of the diverse nature of contemporary societies is considered. This requires sensitive leadership, diplomacy and tact.

 Activity: Develop a safety policy

Consider your organisation. Look at one policy that has been recently adopted, for example web safety. What role did staff, governors and parents have in developing this school policy?

This task illustrates that developing a policy requires open debate. So, one cannot accept policy development uncritically. Its development and journey through discussions will be based on the individual values of different socio-cultural groups. It involves everybody in an organisation and every opinion, no matter how diverse, needs to be considered openly and honestly. Where there are tensions about policy details, seek advice, and where there are tensions of implementation, resolve the issue through internal processes for an amicable outcome. The role of leadership becomes an adversary and enabling one, where they explain their actions. Here, leadership is located in a policy context and may require different leadership styles – autocratic, democratic or situational.

 Reflective question

In what ways are leaders in an organisation both policy implementers and policy generators in shaping policy?

Consider in this reflection how an individual can help shape policy at an early stage. Are you a member of a working group to influence ideas? We suggest that each one of us can act as a change agent in the development of policy. After all, practitioners are, on a daily basis, at the forefront of understanding what education is about, how to implement it, for whom and who decides. These are the core values through which policy develops. The voices of governors are important in developing, monitoring and evaluating school policies. They are accountable for the continuing effectiveness and probity of the schools and now, with little help or advice from LAs, their skills are even more important.

Developing a policy: View from an academy

Case study 2.1: Dale Community Special Education College

Dale Community Special Education College is a large urban academy, and is part of a multi-academy trust, an umbrella trust. It supports improvements to SEN provision and attainment and the well-being of pupils with Special Education Needs. This college has formed collaborations with other partner schools to share resources to best meet the local needs of the communities they serve. School-to school support and collaboration was not an easy activity. It required much diplomacy, tact and give-and-take to get to a win–win situation for each school. Dale Community Special College worked with the staff and governors to be self-managing and to develop a self-improving system. It carefully monitored the effect of this newly created school on the intake and attainment of neighbouring schools and found many wins, having more learners, more quickly and achieving much more.

Case study 2.2: A primary academy

A primary academy trust has the power to change a school's terms and conditions for staff. Governors are aware of the risks, although in reality few academies seem to have used these powers. How can this situation be seen as a positive move, allowing academies greater freedom to reward staff?

These case studies show there are tensions about the functioning of trusts and it is something that needs considering carefully in conjunction with staff. Before, schools could seek support from their Local Authority professional, but now that role has gone and schools must find their own, alternative source of external challenge and support. Academy schools must seek out and purchase their own support. As a stand-alone academy, governors play a vital role in policy development to do with financial planning, curriculum and other education matters, but as part of a multi-academy trust, the ultimate responsibility lays with the multi-academy trust directors.

Summary

This chapter addressed issues about education policy and how leaders and governors manage organisational strategies to promote a high-quality education service to future service users. A range of examples were examined to understand how policy implementation is influenced by many external and internal drivers. The complexity of the governance and accountability agenda discussed shows the need for leaders and governors to work collegially to bring about change by megatrends impacting the education sector. Being aware of the external factors and then maximising the intelligence, ability, skills and knowledge of staff, governors, parents and learners to manage change then becomes less of a daunting challenge.

References

Armstrong, M. (2009) *Armstrong's Handbook of Management and Leadership: A Guide to Managing for Results,* 2nd edn. London: Kogan Page.

Bell, L. and Stevenson, H. (2006) Citizenship and Social Justice: Developing education policy in multi-ethnic schools. In *Education Policy Process, Themes and Impact*. Abingdon: Routledge.

Bottery, M. (2008) How different are we? Globalisation and the perceptions of leadership challenges in England and Hong Kong. *Educationalfutures*, e-journal of the British Education Studies Association, 1 (1), August 2008: 1–15.

Brighouse, T. and Woods, D. (1999) *How to Improve Your School*. London: Routledge.

Bush, T. and Oduro, G. (2006) New principals in Africa: Preparation, induction and practice. *Journal of Educational Administration*, 44 (4): 359–375.

Caldwell, B. J. and Spinks, J. M. (1988) *The Self-Managing School*. Lewes: Falmer Press.

Crow, G. (2006) Complexity and the beginning principal in the United States: Perspectives on socialisation. *Journal of Educational Administration*, 44 (4): 310–325.

De Geus, A. (1997) *The Living Company: Growth, Learning and Longevity in Business.* London: Nicholas Brealey.

Foskett, N. (2002) Marketing. In T. Bush and L. Bell (eds) *The Principles and Practice of Educational Management*. London: Paul Chapman Publishing., pp. 241–257.

Gardner, H. E. (1999) *Intelligence Reframed: Multiple Intelligences for the 21st Century.* New York: Basic Books.

Grint, K. (2005) Problems, problems, problems: The social construction of 'leadership'. *Human Relations*, 58 (11): 1467–1494.

Hallinger, P. (2001) Leading educational change in East Asian schools. *International Studies in Educational Administration,* 29 (2): 61–72.

Handy, C. (1994) *The Empty Raincoat*. London: Hutchison.

Heifetz, R. A. and Linsky, M. (2002) *Leadership on the Line: Staying Alive through the Danger of Leading*. Boston, MA: Harvard Business School Press.

Innovations International. (2016) *Creativity*, http://www.innovint.com/services/creativity_2.php (accessed January 2017).

Johnson, G., Scholes, K. and Whittington, R. (2008) *Exploring Corporate Strategy*. London: Pearson Education.

Kolb, D. A. (1984) *Experiential Learning: Experience as the Source of Learning and Development*. Hemel Hempstead: Prentice-Hall International.

Lumby, J. (2015) *Exploring the Micropolitics of Leadership in Higher Education*. Research Report, July 2015, London: Leadership Foundation for Higher Education.

Marsh, J. (1993) *The Strategic Toolkit*. London: IFS International.

May, A. (2011) Tomorrow will not be the same as today. Power-point presentation by the Corporate Director for Children and Young People, Nottinghamshire County Council to the ALICSE programme. Nottingham: SDSA.

Mistry, M. and Sood, K. (2012) How are leaders integrating the ideology of globalisation in primary school contexts? *Education 3–13: International Journal of Primary, Elementary and Early Years Education*, pp. 1–13, iFirst article.

Munby, S. (2012) Leadership for the future. Presentation to headteachers at Oxford, 21 March 2012. Nottingham: National College.

National College Annual Survey, 2010/11 https://www.gov.uk/government/uploads/system/uploads/attachment_data/file/247375/1153.pdf (accessed April 2016).

Samier, E. (2014) The covert in administration and leadership studies. In E. Samier (ed.) *Secrecy and Tradecraft in Educational Administration*. Abingdon: Routledge, pp. 35–48.

Senge, P. M. (1990) *The Fifth Discipline*. New York: Doubleday.

Senge, P. (1996) *The Fifth Discipline: The Art and Practice of the Learning Organisation*. Sydney: Random House.

West-Burnham, J. (1994) Strategy, policy and planning. In T. Bush and J. West-Burnham (eds) *The Principles of Educational Management*. Harlow: Longman.

Wilkinson, R. and Pickett, K. (2010) *The Spirit Level*. London: The Equality Trust.

Wylie, C. and Mitchell, L. (2003) Sustaining school development in a decentralised system: Lessons from New Zealand. Paper presented at International Congress for School Effectiveness and Improvement, 5–8 January 2003. Sydney: New Zealand Council for Educational Research.

3 Changes to the employment market

Chapter aims

When you have finished reading this chapter you will be able to:

1. explain the importance of an appropriate staffing profile to learning and teaching;
2. discuss some of the pressures and issues regarding staff recruitment;
3. identify options for employing staff in organisations;
4. describe different staff contracts and some of the advantages and disadvantages of each.

Overview of chapter

This chapter examines the employment challenges faced by education leaders in maintaining an appropriately skilled staff team. To meet government attainment targets and to ensure a high-quality learning experience for all, leaders need to be confident they have the right number of appropriately qualified staff in the right roles at the right time. This requires forward and contingency planning from leaders and may require flexibility and/or retraining of staff when new initiatives are introduced or when issues arise which require a swift organisational response. Significant numbers of educators 'leaving the profession' (Syal and Weale, 2016) coupled with many 'unfilled training places' (ibid.) has resulted in 'chronic shortages emerging in some regions and some subjects' (Millar, 2016) creating claims of a 'crisis over … recruitment and retention' (ibid.). Pressure appears to be particularly acute in maths, natural sciences (biology, chemistry and physics) and modern foreign languages. These shortages have placed considerable pressure on education providers and produced a unique set of problems for leaders as they try to locate, recruit, retain and/or retrain staff. As a result of staffing pressures many leaders are forced into making short-term emergency responses and are having to consider creative solutions to meet organisational staffing demands, including looking beyond traditional recruitment routes to fill vacancies.

Key words: employment; recruitment and selection; staffing; training.

Introduction

Education leaders must take ultimate responsibility for leading their organisation. While they may be supported by a governing body or executive team, they are the public face of their organisation and are accountable for the successes (and failures) of their organisation. As an increasing number of organisations are joining together to form federations or alliances, some leaders (namely executive heads or chief executives) are now responsible for a number of organisations. It is the leader's role to create a vision for their organisation(s) and the team(s) who work within them and to plan how their vision will be implemented and achieved.

This chapter explores some of the key employment issues facing leaders in education settings. It examines challenges of recruitment, choices regarding types of employment contracts and options for filling vacancies using home and/or international staff.

National College Framework for Leadership

While not applicable to every sector, the National College for Teaching and Leadership has developed a useful framework, shown in Figure 3.1, which indicates some of the key responsibilities and functions of an education leader when planning staffing teams. Leaders need to make sure they have the requisite staffing profile which ensures they can achieve educational excellence for all learners, guarantee effective operational management of routine tasks and provide visionary strategic leadership to take the organisation forward.

The diagram opposite indicates the complex and multi-faceted role of leading in education. While leaders need to have a good understanding of the different roles in their organisation, they cannot personally (and should not even attempt to) carry out each of these individual roles. Such behaviour would be wasteful of the leader's skills and may demonstrate a lack of confidence or trust in other staff. Leaders should avoid being distracted by the minutiae of daily life in education and recognise that while these issues are significant to individual staff members, it is not the leader's responsibility to intervene and directly solve every problem in an organisation. Ultimately, the leader's primary role is to orchestrate the efforts of others and through structured positive encouragement, enable and empower staff to take control in their working lives, manage workloads and solve emergent challenges. To achieve this task, leaders need to provide strategic direction and professional support to all staff in their work.

Each of the three leadership themes – educational excellence, operational management and strategic leadership – is reliant on the recruitment, selection and retention of suitably qualified team members who have the skills and qualities needed to complete their

Figure 3.1 Key roles of education leaders (adapted from National College for Teaching and Leadership, 2013)

individual roles and to help achieve whole-organisation ambitions. Leaders can only hope to fulfil their role, and achieve their vision for their institution, by working through others and effectively leading their teams.

Reflective questions

1. Thinking about your own organisation, how well do you believe the three separate components of leadership are realised?
2. In your view is any one component significantly weaker than the others?
3. What do you see as the leadership priorities within your organisation? Why do you believe this?

Discussion: Leading for influence

Most leaders will, in common with their staff teams, demonstrate a spiky competence profile and will be demonstrably better at some leadership skills than others. This in itself is not an issue as long as the leader has assembled a sufficiently skilled team to help them carry out all functions. However, as the head of the organisation the leader must take control of the bigger strategic issues and be the driving force behind these initiatives, spearheading organisational change. As a result of needing to control this key responsibility, leaders will have to delegate more routine roles, such as operational management and curriculum issues, to other members of the senior leadership team. However, this action does not minimise the importance of these other leadership tasks and leaders will need to retain a watching brief for both educational excellence and operational management. Should either of these areas start to present challenges, the leader would need to reconsider their priorities and may need to intervene directly to resolve difficult situations.

To enable them to drive organisational change, leaders need to have confidence in the skills and abilities of their senior team. It is only when leaders are sure their wider team can manage that they can comfortably relinquish some of their overall responsibilities. To achieve this position, it is essential leaders have developed a clear succession plan and know to whom they can confidently assign key organisational tasks. As a result leaders must consider the skill set of their executive, senior and middle management teams and devise processes to ensure their management teams are continually developing their individual leadership competencies. Centrally the need to develop the next generation of educational leaders has been recognised by national government who supported the National College to develop a suite of courses to support headship, senior and middle leader roles and train new leaders to service the needs of primary and secondary education. However, effective leadership is needed across all phases of education, from nursery schooling to prison education, prompting Ofsted to report that the best leaders

> have a clear vision of what they are trying to achieve ... [and] are absolutely determined to 'get it right first time' ... They communicate convincingly leading by example [and] never lose sight of the link between the quality of the provision and its impact on ... learning and development.
>
> (Ofsted, 2013: 5)

Contemporary issues in staffing

Maintaining the appropriate balance of staff at all times is one of the most important roles for any leader working in education. Without the appropriate staff, team leaders will be unable to ensure high-quality learning for all. For leaders this means having both the apposite number of staff to fill all positions with the correct qualifications at the required level. However, tales of 'long hours, low starting pay and limited access to professional development' (Sellen, 2016) is making it harder for leaders to fill posts.

Organisations 'with large proportions of disadvantaged pupils find attracting and keeping good teachers' (Burns, 2016) challenging and many schools 'in deprived areas find it difficult to attract and retain teachers' (Prentice, 2016). Teachers in these environments often experience high levels of 'emotional demands … leaving them emotionally exhausted and less satisfied with their work' (Kinman et al., 2011: 850). Tales of constant disruption deter both experienced and newly qualified staff from applying for posts and organisations are left reliant on costly cover staff. At the same time there are reports of many 'experienced teachers leaving the profession' (Moorhead, 2016). This double-ended attrition (low recruitment coupled with high staff turnover) has created a perfect staffing storm and some organisations can barely meet the needs of their learners.

Staffing shortages are particularly acute in areas with a lack of affordable housing. In London and other areas where rents and property prices are high, organisations have persistent unfilled vacancies as many staff cannot afford to live in the area. Even with the additional London allowance (paid on a sliding scale of inner, outer and fringe), accommodation costs remain prohibitively high for many teachers. In a bid to combat difficulties in recruitment some London boroughs (for example Haringey) have chosen to pay staff at the higher inner London rate even though they could legitimately pay the lower outer rate. Further, a number of housing associations including the Peabody Trust, Viridian and Affinity Trust all provide low-cost housing to key workers, including teachers, in areas with high demand. In addition, the Teachers' Housing Association, which is targeted specifically at education workers, provides affordable accommodation in the London boroughs of Bexley, Brent, Croydon, Kingston-on-Thames and Waltham Forest and some education organisations have directly offered housing as part of their employment offer.

On a national level, it has become more difficult to employ staff in some subject areas. Notably 'in secondary schools more classes are being taught by teachers without a relevant post-A-level qualification' (Burns, 2016); and there are 'acute difficulties … in maths, English, science and languages' (ibid.) which has resulted in some children being taught by non-specialist staff.

The Williams Report, which specifically examined the quality of mathematics teaching in primary schools and Early Years, found despite improvements following the introduction of the National Numeracy Strategy in 1999, 'around six percent of all children leave primary school without attaining level 3 in mathematics at Key Stage 2' (DCSF, 2008: 5). Failure to achieve expected standards was in part attributed to a lack of 'deep mathematical subject and pedagogical knowledge' (ibid.: 3) on the part of teachers, prompting the recommendation 'there should be at least one mathematics specialist in each primary school (ibid.: 4). In turn this recommendation produced the Mathematics Specialist Teacher Programme (also known as MAST), a CPD initiative designed to increase the skills level of an existing practitioner to 'champion mathematics … act as mentor and coach, as well as being an outstanding classroom teacher' (ibid.). Other initiatives to try to increase the supply of maths specialists have included enhanced training bursaries, an incentive also offered to secondary science teachers. While the MAST programme has helped to address some of the concerns at the primary level, many secondary schools and Early Years settings still struggle to recruit staff with sufficient skills in mathematics and there is an ongoing shortage of science, English and language specialists. The recruitment problem has become so pronounced that the Association of School and College Leaders (ASCL) believes 'teacher shortages are having a detrimental impact' (ASCL, 2016) on learning and in a recent survey of 4,000 teachers 70 per cent believed the 'recruitment crisis was affecting pupils' achievement (Moorhead, 2016).

Case study 3.1: Filling the gap

Following the retirement of her deputy, Jane, the headteacher of a primary school, was left with a significant gap in her staff team. Not only had Jane lost a senior leader but the retired deputy had also been her maths specialist. Jane now had a team of mostly newly qualified staff. Although Jane had tried to succession plan by identifying staff who might be future leaders, she did not feel any staff were yet ready for this responsibility. Further, no-one was willing to study the MAST programme, with them all stating they felt they were 'too new to the role' to take on other responsibilities.

Reflective questions

1. What are Jane's priorities/options in this situation?
2. What are the opportunities/threats presented by this situation?
3. What support does Jane need at this time?

Discussion: Leading from the front

One of the responsibilities of a leader is to take charge of difficult situations. Losing both a senior leader and a subject specialist at the same time means Jane now has a number of immediate challenges.

In the first instance Jane must seek the support and guidance of her governing body. While it is likely the governors will be generally aware of the issues, Jane needs to make sure they are fully apprised of the details including the potential impact of losing a subject specialist on educational excellence and pupil attainment. With the support of her governors, Jane needs to devise an immediate short-term response and a longer-term plan to address this situation. Jane also needs to seek the support of her staff team and to keep them informed of developments.

To cover immediate staffing gaps Jane may need to use agency or cover staff, which might be a useful means of locating potential future candidates. Alternatively, if she employs higher-level teaching assistants, it is possible some of them may be able to help with short-term class cover. If Jane has a non-teaching role she could consider undertaking some teaching duties herself on a short-term basis. As Jane and her governors develop a strategic response, the current teaching team may be asked to temporarily take on new or additional roles and Jane could use her deputy's departure as an opportunity to locate, nurture or grow home-grown talent. While some of her team have expressed reluctance to take on new challenges, having experienced a temporary post they may be willing to continue in this role. However, to prevent claims of bias there needs to be transparency in this process. Even though it could be tempting to try to appoint quickly to solve the immediate staffing issues, it may be better to invest in comprehensive recruitment strategies to secure the best candidate possible, even though this may take longer.

When staff leave, rather than immediately seeking to replace like with like, Jane and her governing body should carefully re-examine the institutional needs. Although it is likely key institutional roles as a maths leader and a deputy would need to be replaced, this may not always be the case and vacancies may enable a reconfiguration of existing responsibilities and roles. Rather than having a single deputy, Jane could consider having a number of middle leaders who shared management responsibility. In this way, Jane would have helped to provide greater management security as she would have a number of junior leaders she could turn to for future support. It would be particularly important to carry out a staffing evaluation exercise if there was a predicted fall in the number on the school roll.

Recruiting and managing staff

While many Early Years providers operate year-round, often only closing for statutory and bank holidays, most schools and colleges are tied into an annual recruitment cycle with the academic year starting in the autumn and running through to the summer. Although governing bodies are responsible for deciding the number of staff needed and the salary grade for appointments, it is the organisation's leader who is responsible for determining the staffing plan based on local needs. Many leaders aim to have a full staffing profile in place for the start of the academic year which forms a natural starting point to begin initiatives and gives a complete academic year to embed and evaluate any new procedures.

Organisation leaders are further responsible for managing the appointment process including producing job descriptions and person specifications for roles, advertising posts and interviewing candidates. Once in post, education leaders are ultimately responsible for all aspects of an employee's work including: coordinating new starters' induction plans; ensuring proper professional standards are achieved and maintained; allocation of duties and day-to-day management of tasks; and regular appraisal of work. The leader must also satisfy the governing body that staffing costs remain within designated budgetary limits. While it may be tempting to enhance salary grades for difficult-to-fill positions, this is not possible unless it has been expressly agreed and approved by the governing body. Currently, for most types of permanent teaching and learning posts from Early Years through to further education, employees are required to work some sort of probation period. Renewal of contract is dependent on successful completion of probation. The length and terms and conditions of a probation period will vary from setting to setting.

Staff contracts

In agreement with their governing body, leaders are able to utilise a range of different staffing contracts, some of which are shown in Table 3.1. While there is considerable local variation in employment, typically a full-time teaching contract is for 1,265 annualised hours over a 39-week period, which equates to just over 32 hours per week, although many teachers work more than this in order to meet the requirements of the role. Indeed, recent survey data suggests 'full-time teachers in secondary schools in England now work an average of 48.2 hours per week … 19% longer than the OECD average' (Sellen, 2016). Permanent and temporary contracts may either be full or part time. Part-time contracts may vary from 0.1 (half a day per week) to 0.9 (4.5 days per week).

Leaders need to consider what types of staff contracts best meet the needs of their organisation. This means having a good understanding of the existing population of learners and local demographics which could indicate changes in overall learner numbers or the number of particular types of learner. For example, a proposed closure of a neighbouring school could create a sudden rise in intake; the area may have a significant population of learners with EAL; or as a result of decline in local industry and outward migration of associated workers and their families there may be an ongoing fall in learner recruitment. Any of these situations can create either a staffing surplus or shortage and leaders need to manage this situation.

Often, leaders use supply staff to cover short-term shortages or may use fixed-term contracts. Surpluses may involve internal redeployment of staff or could mean potential redundancies. Leaders also need to be mindful of the internal environment and be aware of who may be approaching retirement or staff who may be seeking to take parental/adoption leave or meet other caring commitments. Most education organisations can expect some degree of staff turnover resulting in a continuous cycle of recruitment – this is normal for any large organisation. However, leaders need to be mindful of institutional stability and high levels of staff turnover may threaten organisationalconstancy and may be indicative of staff dissatisfaction or poor institutional health. Losing a permanent member of staff provides an opportunity to review how staffing needs are met and leaders will need to consider if they

Table 3.1 Types of staffing contract

Type of contract	Suitable for	Arrangements for ending contract
Permanent	This type of contract should be offered where there is a permanent continuing post, for example a Key Stage 1 class teacher in a primary school. This type of contract is in wide usage.	Normally an employee would be required to work a notice period before leaving. This would usually be about a term (8–12 weeks) to enable the employer to advertise for a replacement. If an employee has failed to improve after warning, an employer can terminate a contract due to unsatisfactory performance.
Fixed-term temporary	This may be offered if employment is for a set period, for example to cover maternity leave. Notice of end date is usually served on appointment. This type of contract is in wide use.	If the end date has been notified in advance, no further action is needed by the employer.
Open-ended temporary	This is suitable when the end date is not known or cannot be reasonably predicted, for example to cover illness. This type of contract is not very common.	Termination of contract is based on the appropriate statutory or contractual entitlement, whichever is the greater.
Supply/ sessional/ casual	These types of contract are common in education and provide both employee and employer with flexibility without the commitment and responsibilities of permanent roles. They can vary from daily roles to longer posts. The level of responsibility usually increases depending on the time spent in the setting.	The likely end date of employment is usually known in advance by the employee and no further action is required by the employer.
Zero-hour contracts	Currently 'nearly one in four businesses in the education sector' (Dickens, 2016) use these contracts. This type of contract is most common for supply teachers and ancillary workers. The usage of these contracts is not clear.	As the employee has no guarantee of employment, no notice of termination is required by the employer.

need another permanent contract or if hours could be disaggregated into a number of part-time roles.

International staff

To meet staffing demands, some leaders may want to consider recruiting staff from overseas. However, it is important that leaders are aware there are different rules for employing staff who qualified outside the UK regarding the type of contract that can be offered and the teacher's length of stay. This is sometimes referred to as 'the four-year rule'. In summary:

> teachers who qualified outside of the European Economic Alliance (EEA) and Switzerland having successfully completed a course of initial teacher training which is recognised by the relevant authorities in their home countries … [may] teach in state

maintained schools and non-maintained special schools in England as unqualified teachers for four calendar years. Teachers who qualified in Australia, Canada, New Zealand and the United States of America (USA) may apply for QTS without further training or assessment in England.

(DfE, 2014: 3)

During this four-year period international staff are expected to work towards gaining QTS by following a recognised programme of study. Overseas candidates who have previously qualified as a teacher in their home country may be able to use their previous experience to help them access either school- or university-led training programmes. Some universities recognise such previous achievement and candidates are able to use their experience to help them complete aspects of their teacher training courses. Trainees need to carefully research all options available to determine the most appropriate route into teaching for them and there are many different options including full-time, part-time, distance and online courses. As an overseas candidate, however, it may be necessary to apply for a visa before beginning any training course. Although requirements for training courses can vary slightly from provider to provider, most courses require the equivalent of a UK first degree; a GCSE grade C or above in Maths and English; and a GCSE grade C or above in Science to teach in primary or Key Stage 2/3. Many courses will also expect some placement experience in a school or other suitable setting. Qualification equivalence can be checked via the National Academic Recognition Information Centre (also known as NARIC) for a fee. Until successfully achieving QTS, overseas candidates are paid as unqualified staff.

Case study 3.2: Employing staff

After being unable to successfully fill a staff vacancy for two years, Sandra, a primary headteacher in a busy urban area, had relied on using expensive agency staff to ensure the day-to-day running of her school. In order to try to reduce her dependency on temporary staff and reduce costs, Sandra decided to explore other options.

After investigation she found she could employ an overseas candidate for up to four years. Sandra was very excited about this prospect, feeling an overseas trained teacher could bring new perspectives and would allow the students to meet someone who had a different life experience. She discussed this matter initially with the school governors and then her school leadership team before presenting the proposal to the whole staff. All groups received the suggestion positively and believed the children would benefit from greater stability in the teaching team. Although appointment conditions would be different and the overseas teacher could only be employed as an unqualified teacher while he/she worked towards gaining QTS, after so much uncertainty Sandra was committed to pursuing this option and hoped over time she would be able to support the successful candidate to gain full QTS via one of the part-time distance learning options.

Working with her chair of governors, Sandra was able to appoint a qualified teacher from Cameroon. The candidate began work and everything seemed to be going well. However, Sandra has received a letter from a parent asking why the school has to employ 'foreigners' and could the school not find 'any English teachers'. The parent further alleges the teacher 'cannot speak English very well' and they are worried this will have a detrimental impact on their child's education. The parent has also suggested a number of other parents are unhappy and hold the same views.

Reflective questions

1. What staffing issues are you aware of in your setting? Are there any unfilled vacancies? If so, how long have these posts been vacant?
2. What recruitment strategies are used to find staff? Where does your organisation advertise to find employees? Is your organisation making full use of online platforms and other forms of media to help fill staff vacancies?
3. How does your setting announce new staff appointments to families?

Discussion: Filling vacancies

When seeking to fill vacancies, it is sometimes necessary for education leaders to think creatively. While it is possible that traditional recruitment methods, such as local and national education press or online advertising, may produce positive results, some employers now need to extend their recruitment strategies. In a bid to fill vacancies, some organisations have formed productive networks with local community groups and training providers including FE colleges and universities. Working with these groups, education settings have given prior notice of forthcoming vacancies and may even provide work experience opportunities to help candidates make the best application possible. While employing overseas tutors may not be the first option for all organisations, it has considerable advantages. Organisations will immediately gain an experienced member of staff who could also help promote global education initiatives, with the further potential of international networking. However, it is important that international tutors are properly supported should they be appointed. This might include an induction period prior to beginning employment to introduce the new member of staff to organisational practice or local idiosyncrasies and will probably need to include ongoing pastoral and/or academic support once in post.

Case study 3.2 highlights that not all members of an education community may welcome overseas trained teachers and the teacher in this scenario has attracted implicitly racist comments from a parent. In this situation Sandra, in her role as headteacher, needs to respond. In the first instance the appointed teacher should be supported as long as he or she is performing to required standards and should not be made to feel responsible for the intolerant attitudes of others. In this case Sandra needs to operate standard school procedures: if her school would usually notify parents of new staff appointments, this practice should be followed; if not, then no action should be taken. It is important the overseas teacher should not be seen as or treated as some kind of novelty.

In order to clarify the position and to check if more parents are unhappy with the decision to appoint an overseas teacher, Sandra may wish to invite the dissatisfied parent into school for a discussion. In this conversation, without being defensive, Sandra needs to reaffirm her professional responsibilities as a headteacher to make staff appointments. Sandra should try to explore the background behind events that led to this parent's comments: Was there a particular issue which had caused concern? Had their child informed the family of a notable incident? However, it is important Sandra informs the parent that as long as staff are working at the required level and there are no issues regarding professional competence, they are guaranteed institutional support from both the headteacher and the governing body. She may also want to inform the parent of the requirements of the 2010 Equality Act and how racism of any kind is not tolerated in the school environment.

Summary

In this chapter we have examined the ethical difficulties and dilemmas leaders face when working to ensure they have a well-qualified staff team able to meet the needs of all learners in their care. Although leaders are the figurehead of an establishment, they need to remember that they, too, are part of a number of teams, including the governance team, the leadership team and the whole staff team, and will need to work with these various teams in different ways at different times. Ultimately, the success of the organisation depends on the effectiveness of the staff team and, as the proverb states, each team is only as strong as its weakest link. It is the role of the leader to help every link to be as strong as possible.

In order to make their institutional vision a reality, leaders may need to build new teams to help them achieve that vision. This will require robust selection procedures which enable the most appropriately skilled staff to be recruited. When experiencing difficulties in filling roles, leaders should be prepared to think creatively and explore new avenues. Leaders may sometimes need to adopt a tiered approach which enables them to address immediate concerns while maintaining sufficient flexibility to accommodate future issues. This could involve using a variety of staffing contracts to service organisational requirements. However, many leaders inherit teams and in order to achieve institutional goals will need to widen their existing staff's skill base through structured development and training programmes.

It is important when leading their organisations that leaders maintain a clear overview of institutional needs at all times so they can direct operations to drive forward strategic initiatives, maintain operational standards and support educational excellence. Such a foresighted tactical approach, which maintains the needs of the organisation at its core, is the essence of educational leadership.

References

Association of School and College Leaders (ASCL) (2016) Survey shows damage of teacher shortages. Available at http://www.ascl.org.uk/news-and-views/news_news-detail.survey-shows-damage-of-teacher-shortages.hyml (accessed 28 October 2016).

Burns, J. (2016) Teacher shortages in england, spending watchdog confirms. BBC. Available at http://www.bbc.co.uk/news/education-35531982 (accessed 28 October 2016).

Department for Children, Schools and Families (DCSF) (2008) *Independent Review of Mathematics Teaching in Early Years Settings and Primary Schools.* Nottingham: DCSF Publications. Available at http://www.catchuo.org/resources/605/independent_review_of_mathematics_teaching_in_early_years_settings_and_primary_schools.pdf (accessed 4 December 2016).

Department for Education (DfE) (2014) *Overseas Trained Teachers – Departmental Advice for Overseas Trained Teachers, Local Authorities, Maintained Schools and Governing Bodies.* Available at https://www.gov.uk/government/uploads/system/uploads/attachment_data/file/387894/OTTs_web_guidance_10_Dec_14.pdf (accessed 11 December 2016).

Dickens, J. (2015) Zero-hour contracts increase in education sector. *Schools Week*, 11 September. Available at http://schoolsweek.co.uk/zero-hours-contracts-escalate-in-education/ (accessed 30 October 2016).

Kinman, G., Wray, S. and Strange, C. (2011) Emotional labour, burnout and job satisfaction in UK teachers: The role of workplace social support. *Educational Psychology,* 31 (7): 843–856.

Millar, F. (2016) Teacher recruitment 'a mess' as every school slugs it out for itself. *Guardian*, 19 January 2016. Available at https://www.theguardian.com/education/2016/jan/19/teacher-recruitment-school-shortages (accessed 29 October 2016).

Moorhead, J. (2016) Schools are relying on inexperienced staff and supply teachers survey reveals. *Guardian*, 22 March 2016. Available at https://www.theguardian.com/teacher-network/2016/mar/22/schools-are-relying-on-inexperienced-staff-and-supply-teachers-survey-reveals (accessed 1 November 2016).

National College for Teaching and Leadership (2013) *National College for Teaching and Leadership's Leadership Curriculum,* Available at http://www.lcll.org.uk/uploads/2/1/4/7/21470046/trainee_headteacher_handbook_npqh_2013.pdf (accessed 30 October 2016).

Ofsted (2013) *Getting It Right First Time – Achieving and Maintaining High-Quality Early Years Provision.* Manchester: Ofsted, Available at https://www.gov.uk/government/publications/achieving-and-maintaining-high-quality-early-years-proviion-getting-it-right-first-time (accessed 30 November 2016).

Prentice. C. (2016) How can we combat the teaching shortage in deprived areas? *Guardian*, 5 August 2016. Available at https://www.theguardian.com/teacher-network/2016/aug/05/how-can-we-combat-the-teacher-shortage-in-deprived-areas (accessed 4 December 2016).

Sellen, P. (2016) Long hours and low pay: Why England's teachers face burnout. *Guardian,* 11 October 2016. Available at https://www.theguardian.com/teacher-network/2016/oct/11/teachers-reeling-under-massive-workload-report (accessed 28 October 2016).

Syal, R. and Weale, S. (2016) Teachers are leaving as government falls short on recruitment, NAO finds. *Guardian*, 10 February 2016. Available at https://www.theguardian.com/education/2016/feb/10/teachers-are-leaving-as-government-falls-short-on-recruitment-nao-finds (accessed 30 October 2016).

4 Inclusion in education, emerging moral dilemmas and legislative changes

Chapter aims

When you have finished reading this chapter you will be able to:

1. explain to young people, local community members (including parents and carers), internal and external education professionals and other non-specialist groups what inclusion means to you personally and for your organisation in your leadership role;
2. identify how your organisation works to achieve inclusion of *all* students and staff and provide specific examples of actions you have taken as a leader to support and promote inclusion in your setting;
3. state what moral issues have arisen for you personally, for your organisation and how, as a leader, you have managed these concerns to produce positive outcomes for all parties;
4. list how practice and/or procedures have changed in your organisation as a result of legislation.

Overview of the chapter

This chapter explores how, in a climate of constant change and challenging new legal responsibilities, by creating inclusive learning environments education leaders can better enable learners to reach their potential through utilising the talents of all their staff. We begin the chapter by providing a brief historical context of selected equality legislation in the UK before considering what inclusion in education means through the lens of the 2010 Equality Act and the statutory 2015 Special Educational Needs and Disability Code of Practice. We examine actions leaders need to take to create inclusive learning environments and the impact of the Equality Act for staff, students and communities. Next we consider the need for moral leadership in creating a vision based on ethical values to meet present and future needs of communities, through positive staff engagement. Finally, we examine the implications of working ethically with children, young people and staff and how by having high expectations, the whole learning community can become a force for change.

Key words: equality; inclusion; legislation; moral leadership; sustainability.

Introduction

Education leaders are ultimately responsible for creating an environment which allows each young person to achieve her or his potential. This incorporates educational attainment as measured by external tests (for example Early Years Developmental Milestones, Key Stage 2 SATs or GCSEs) and other recognised assessments, in addition to broader outcomes including personal health, emotional well-being and ultimately employment opportunities. Education leaders in the twenty-first century will need to manage these challenges through working with a more diverse workforce employed on a wider range of contracts, supporting a greater range of educational needs. To promote inclusion of learners and workers in rapidly changing fluid situations, leaders will need to develop a coherent, persuasive vision to secure the support of internal and external communities. Leaders need a clear sense of purpose to confront challenging moral dilemmas and meet their legal obligations. Achieving educational inclusion for learning communities means working differently and narrow operational practices of the past will not support this goal. Leaders will need to work with traditional partners such as community associations and Local Authorities (LAs) and extend their networks to make full use of other supportive public and voluntary organisations.

Inclusion in education

The UK has a chequered history of supporting inclusion and equality. Historically, it was an enthusiastic supporter of the trans-Atlantic slave trade, yet abolished slavery in 1807 over 50 years before the USA which took until 1865 to officially end the practice. In contrast, in recent times the UK introduced sex and race discrimination legislation in 1975 and 1976 respectively, approximately ten years behind the USA. Similarly in education, the USA passed its landmark 'No Child Left Behind' Act in 2001, two years before the UK's comparable 2003 'Every Child Matters' Act. Both Acts sought to reduce ingrained structural educational disadvantage, put in place measures which would allow all children to thrive in education and provide additional support to those who had traditionally underachieved or were disadvantaged in education. Thus while the UK positions itself as an advocate of equality, it sometimes appears slow in turning theory into practice and making political claims a reality.

In the UK there is a 'broad understanding of equality ... [which] informs many state systems of schooling' (Terzi, 2008: 1) and 'the dominant understanding of educational equality in contemporary Anglo-American political discourse is meritocratic' (Brighouse et al., 2010: 27). While all mainstream political groups appear to agree on the broad principles of equality and inclusion, 'some groups, it seems, are positively disadvantaged by the education system' (Peart, 2013: 3). According to Gillborn, for certain groups failure in education is 'inevitable and permanent under current circumstances' (2008: 45). For example, those with 'Pakistani, Bangladeshi, Black Caribbean, Black African, Black Other and Dual Heritage (White/Black Caribbean) backgrounds' (ibid.: 56) are more likely to fail than their white peers of the same gender and socio-economic status. Similarly, in her research Gunter found 'a general achievement gap for African-Caribbean pupils; Pakistani and Bangladeshi heritage pupils … and children with special needs' (2006: 61). Ofsted also noted that disabled pupils were 'much more likely to be … excluded from school and achieve less well than their peers both in terms of their attainment at any given age and in terms of their progress over time' (2010: 5). For these learners, rather than promoting fairness, education seems to contribute to existing social inequalities.

Although these groups do not seem to fare well in education it is important to remember education is a significant 'mediating factor between the disadvantage experienced' (Dyson, 2006: 119) and later life outcomes. Because compulsory education begins after a child's fifth birthday and continues until the child becomes 16 (after 16 a young person may leave school but must remain in education, employment or training until 18) in the UK, most children spend at least 11 years in education. Consequently education is ideally placed to 'intervene in the reproduction of disadvantage so as to equalize life chances between individuals from different … backgrounds' (ibid.). Current and aspirant education leaders are charged with promoting equality and removing (or at least reducing) prejudicial practices so that all learners have the best possible chance of positive life outcomes. This challenge has been reinforced by the 2010 Equality Act which was designed to eradicate inequality in every area of society including education. Public-sector organisations were required to implement the Act in its entirety, which 'replaced nine major Acts of Parliament and almost a hundred sets of regulations … [and] provided a single consolidated source of discrimination law, covering all the types of discrimination that are unlawful' (DfE, 2014: 7).

The Act identified seven different features relevant to education (known as protected characteristics) and explicitly made discrimination against a student and/or their families unlawful on the grounds of sex, race, disability, religion or belief, sexual orientation, gender reassignment, pregnancy or maternity. Two further protected characteristics, not directly relevant to education – age, and marriage or civil partnership – were also included in the Act. Public-sector organisations were directed to work proactively to:

- Eliminate discrimination and other conduct that is prohibited by the Act;
- Advance equality of opportunity between people who share a protected characteristic and people who do not share it;
- Foster good relations across all characteristics between people who share a protected characteristic and people who do not share it.

(Equality and Human Rights Commission)

Achieving the aims of the Act is embedded in the contractual obligations of all education leaders and head teachers as a result of their leadership role.

On one level, these robust duties seemed to strengthen equality legislation and indeed the Act 'recognised in the advancement of equality' (Peart, 2014: 29) that organisations could, in certain circumstances, implement positive action measures 'to alleviate disadvantages experienced by, or to meet the particular needs of, pupils with particular protected characteristics' (DfE, 2014: 6). However, simultaneously the Act expressly did not cover 'the relationship between one pupil and another … [and did not] … bear directly on such issues as racist or homophobic bullying by pupils' (ibid.: 8), confining its scope to bigger meta-level rather than local meso- or micro-level issues, creating a perceptible distance between theory and praxis. This noticeable separation between policy aims and working practice seemed to preserve confusions created by previous legislation and, to an extent, appeared to weaken leaders' compulsory duties so that once again education leaders were left to work out their own interpretations of the law.

Inclusion for disabled children and young people

While the Act appeared ambiguous in promoting equality in some areas such as race and sexual orientation, it was more robust in protecting the rights of disabled students. Department for Education guidance made it clear that 'schools are allowed to treat disabled pupils more favourably than non-disabled pupils and in some cases are required to do so, by making reasonable adjustments to put them on a more level footing with pupils without disabilities' (DfE, 2014: 11).

Responsibilities towards disabled pupils were further clarified by the 2015 Special Educational Needs and Disability Code of Practice. This statutory Code strengthened existing provisions and raised the standard of 'educational provision and … care that must be achieved for all children and young people with a disability or SEN' (Ruebain and Peart, 2016: 146). Under the Code, a child identified as having SEN and needing 'additional or different educational provision' (ibid.) must have an Education, Health and Care (EHC) plan. The EHC plan replaced SEN statements.

The EHC plan covers a child's entire educational career from birth to 25 years and thus includes all education sectors from Early Years through to further and higher education so preserving continuity and coherence. EHC plans require education providers to work with other relevant organisations such as social services 'to provide comprehensive support so that individuals can realise their potential and make a successful transition into adulthood with the best possible outcomes' (ibid.: 147). Under the new Code services could no longer work in isolation, which had previously created an ad hoc approach to young people's education. Although the DfE believed 'the majority of children and young people with SEN or disabilities [would] have their needs met within local mainstream early years settings, schools or colleges' (DfE, 2015: 142), where a young person had complex or additional needs which could not be realistically met by usual mainstream resources, an EHC plan had to be drawn up. Significantly, 'once a mainstream provider [was] named on an EHC plan' (Ruebain and Peart, 2016: 151), the child or young person has to be admitted to that setting.

In the event of a dispute between the education provider and the family regarding implementation of the EHC plan, the family can appeal to an independent 'disagreement resolution service' (DfE, 2015: 248). If the parties are unable to reach agreement the dispute could be referred onto mediation services and ultimately could be heard by a Special Educational Needs and Disability Tribunal (SENDIST). SENDIST has the authority 'to dismiss the appeal if they find it is not justified; instruct the LA to complete an EHC assessment; direct the LA to draw up an EHC plan; amend an existing EHC plan or order additions; and correct omissions or weaknesses' (Ruebain and Peart, 2016: 153).

Reflective questions

1. What is your current knowledge of equality legislation and statutory codes of practice?
2. How has legislation and your working environment shaped your personal understanding of inclusion?
3. How have you, in your leadership role, responded to legislation and promoted inclusion in your setting?

Discussion: Legislative obligations of leaders

Education leaders are obliged to understand contemporary legislation and how it relates to their individual setting. Although both the 2010 Equality Act and 2015 Special Educational Needs and Disability Code of Practice apply to all settings, the emphasis of the specific measures contained in the statutes will vary according to the sector. For example, in a FE college where many young people are becoming aware of their own sexuality it would be appropriate to facilitate a LGBT (Lesbian, Gay, Bisexual and Transgender) student group. Such a group would not be relevant in a primary school where all students are under the legal age of consent. However, if a primary school has decided to teach sex education, it would be important to discuss different forms of sexuality. When sex education should be taught in the UK remains an unresolved debate, although in 2015 a Commons Education Select Committee 'called for sex and relationships education to be placed on the national curriculum for the first time – making it a statutory requirement in all state primary and secondary schools' (Riley-Smith, 2015). Should the advice of the Select Committee be adopted at some stage, leaders in primary schools would need to specifically consider how they proposed to include discussions on different forms of sexuality.

Everyone has a personal set of values and beliefs which inform how they act. Even though there is no legislation to challenge how individuals may think or feel, education leaders must ensure their actions are wholly consistent with the law even if it is contrary to their personal beliefs. For example a teacher employed in a Christian, Islamic or Jewish school could not during the course of their work publicly condemn same sex marriage as evil and contrary to the will of God. Leaders need to ensure all staff members including teachers, non-teaching and support staff act appropriately and do not express personal discriminatory views to students, parents or carers.

Case study 4.1: Working with students with SEN

Amy Smith has autism and an EHC plan. Both Amy and her family were pleased that she was accepted at an outstanding local academy for the start of the school year in September. Even though the academy was about five miles away from her home, it was Amy's first choice and the family had worked hard with both the primary school and the academy to ensure a smooth transition to secondary education. This had included familiarisation visits to meet the staff and tours of the premises to help Amy settle in when she joined. The academy chosen by Amy and her family was named on her EHC plan.

In May, shortly before the end of the school year, the family received a letter informing them that Amy would not be able to attend the academy and instead would be bused (together with a number of other children with SEN) to another centre in the academy trust. The academy stated that Amy could not be accommodated as originally planned as they had reached capacity to teach pupils with SEN. The academy assured the family the change would not negatively impact on Amy and many of the teachers who would have taught their daughter would also be travelling to the other centre to teach, thus ensuring continuity. Amy's family were angry and upset by the academy's actions which they believed were illegal, contrary to the 2010 Equality Act and the 2015 Special Educational Needs and Disability Code of Practice.

 **Reflective questions**

1. From your understanding of contemporary equality law, what can Amy's family do to challenge the decision of the academy?
2. Do the actions of the academy appear to comply with equality legalisation?
3. What is the process in your setting for supporting children and young people with an EHC plan?

Q Discussion: Meeting the needs of students with SEN

Moving to secondary education is an important stage in a child's education. Most children will be anxious about making this transition. For some children, such as those with autism, the inevitable change in stability and routines may be even more difficult. The purpose of an EHC plan is to ensure a child has the best possible experience and potential difficulties are minimised or removed. If any named party digresses from the agreed course of action, the family has the right to challenge and appeal those decisions. Due process must be followed and in the first instance Amy's family would need to refer matters to the LA dispute resolution service to try to broker an agreement. If this was unsuccessful the matter could be referred to mediation and ultimately to a SENDIST.

Under the 2015 Code of Practice all education providers including independent, state, free schools, academies and academy trusts must honour the school named in the EHC plan. As academy trusts are sometimes groups of organisations who are linked together by formal agreement, trusts may argue equal provision throughout the trust, so that pupils may be taught at one or more sites. Critically only one organisation (and by implication only one site) was named on Amy's EHC plan, and as far as Amy's family were concerned that was the school she would start at in September. The situation has been further complicated by the information that only students with SEN would be bused to the alternative site, which may amount to disability discrimination and the family could appeal the school's decision. Because the Equality Act and the complementary SEN Code of Practice are 'still relatively recent' statutes (Ruebain and Peart, 2016: 154), there is little current case law to set precedence. However, this case study raises some key questions on what education settings can and cannot legally do when working with disabled students and the academy has appeared to show little regard for Amy's wishes. In the absence of case law to determine practice, a case like this would be referred to a SENDIST for decision.

Leadership and creating a sustainable ethical vision

Schools, colleges and other education settings are part of wider local, national and international communities and have responsibilities towards the many different groups which make up these communities. Because contemporary 'developed and industrialised societies tend to be culturally diverse, embracing many subcultures' (Dimmock and Walker, 2005: 9), it is important that education leaders are 'aware of the bigger picture' (Fullan, 2003: 50). Leaders must understand their diverse communities so they can offer a tailored provision which accurately reflects the local context and meets broader national aims in a 'system where all students learn, the gap between high and low performance becomes greatly reduced, and what people learn enables them to become successful citizens and workers' (ibid.: 29).

When introducing or developing and implementing an idea, leaders need a strong sense of purpose – a vision which will benefit the whole community and support greater attainment, fulfilment and enjoyment. Learners and staff *must* observe equality legislation: compliance is not optional. However, to build and sustain an ethical vision of the future where success is assured, leaders need to create a 'culture of commitment' (ibid.: 44), from teachers to technicians, cooks to caretakers, students to supply staff. Making a vision happen requires dedication and leaders need to win the logic and emotion debate, appealing to both reason and passions. Members of the education community must want the vision to become reality and be prepared to work to achieve this, even in the face of potential opposition or challenges, under the leader's direction.

To effectively promote ideas leaders have to understand their internal and external communities. They need to know the history of an organisation: what initiatives were previously tried; how these were received; were earlier schemes successful; or were there blockages? Leaders should not be held hostage to the past or afraid to try ideas which may seem culturally incompatible, but equally should be mindful of tradition and respectful of customs, and use this information to help them design a morally driven vision which has the best prospect of success. Staff, student and community groups are key in this endeavour. If staff have shown resistance, what were the causes of their reluctance? If fears were logistical, what could leaders have put in place or done differently to alleviate concerns? If qualms were ideological or value based, how could leaders have engaged with discussions to explore these and have tough conversations about the new vision? If the challenge lay beyond the organisation, how had leaders worked to build bridges and discover why plans were opposed? Leaders should use all available allies to help them promote their idea and remember the important role students and local community members have in building support.

As well as creating a shared vision, leaders must show a willingness to evaluate ideas and actively seek feedback to improve practice. It is difficult for staff teams to back implementation if they do not feel part of the plan. If ideas are not truly supported they can be easily derailed. Beyond implementation leaders need to devise evaluation strategies for

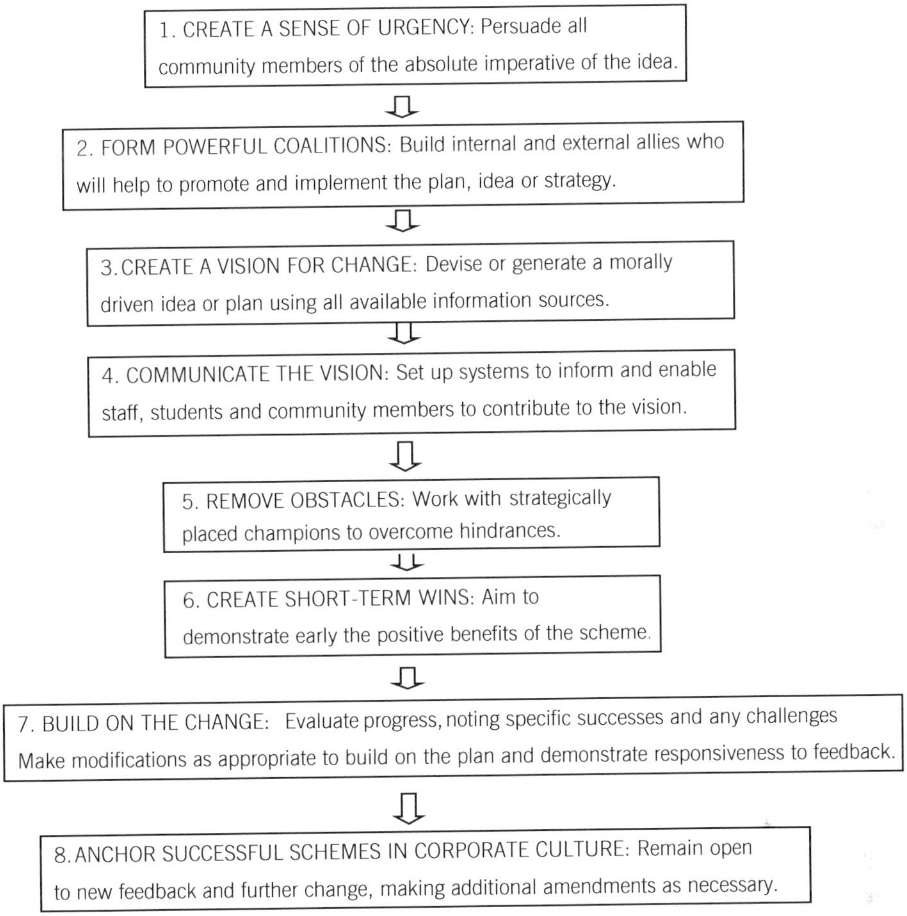

1. CREATE A SENSE OF URGENCY: Persuade all community members of the absolute imperative of the idea.

⇩

2. FORM POWERFUL COALITIONS: Build internal and external allies who will help to promote and implement the plan, idea or strategy.

⇩

3. CREATE A VISION FOR CHANGE: Devise or generate a morally driven idea or plan using all available information sources.

⇩

4. COMMUNICATE THE VISION: Set up systems to inform and enable staff, students and community members to contribute to the vision.

⇩

5. REMOVE OBSTACLES: Work with strategically placed champions to overcome hindrances.

⇩

6. CREATE SHORT-TERM WINS: Aim to demonstrate early the positive benefits of the scheme.

⇩

7. BUILD ON THE CHANGE: Evaluate progress, noting specific successes and any challenges Make modifications as appropriate to build on the plan and demonstrate responsiveness to feedback.

⇩

8. ANCHOR SUCCESSFUL SCHEMES IN CORPORATE CULTURE: Remain open to new feedback and further change, making additional amendments as necessary.

Figure 4.1 Schema for vision implementation (adapted from Kotter, 2012: 37–169)

further development, succession or exit planning. Leaders should not be so wedded to an ideology, flogging the proverbial 'dead horse', that they cannot let go of a proposal or accept when change is necessary. Effective leaders are responsive to prevailing situations and use all available data to help them produce enhanced outcomes.

In this endeavour, 'Lewin's 3 step change model (1951) of Unfreezing, Movement and Refreezing' (Manchester et al., 2014: 82) is helpful. Unfreezing provides a mechanism for examining current practice and introducing 'new protocols to allow for new practice' (ibid.: 85) in a non-judgemental way. Once the blockages are understood, leaders can support staff to take on new procedures and shift organisational culture to embrace the new way of working, before embedding, or 'refreezing' the practice into standard working procedures. In this way both organisational culture and practice can be changed.

Alternatively, leaders could usefully consider Kotter's (1996) more detailed change management model (shown in Figure 4.1) to help support an initiative. This model provides more opportunities to explore staff or community motivations and to persuade them of the need for movement.

Case study 4.2: Changing the teaching timetable

Ian had recently been appointed as head of a small primary school. The previous headteacher was well liked by the staff. The school had a two-form entry with approximately 25 pupils in each class from Years 1 to 6 (NOR circa 300). The policy of the county was to take pupils after their fifth birthday and there was no Reception provision. Ian had a close-knit teaching team of 12 teaching staff including his deputy, who taught a full timetable, and two senior leaders (heads of Key Stages 1 and 2), complemented by a number of teaching assistants (TAs). TAs sometimes taught classes to release the management team or other teachers. Many of the teachers and TAs had worked together for a long time and appeared comfortable in their routines.

The demographics of the school had been changing for some time, largely as a consequence of growing Black African and Indian populations who had either moved into catchment or elected to send their children to the school. There were now 24 children (approximately 8 per cent of the school population) from these two groups. To recognise the changes in the school community, Ian planned to introduce a 'Values Week' for all year groups where different global customs would be discussed and explored through the standard curriculum. Values Week would be taught at the start of the following academic year. For this week teaching would be delivered via a unifying topic-based approach. Ian (who had previously discussed the idea with his deputy) introduced the plan at a whole staff meeting, including TAs and others, explaining he felt it was a good way to reflect the changes in the school community, create a more welcoming environment and reinvigorate the curriculum. About a week after the staff meeting, the Key Stage 1 senior leader approached Ian saying four teachers and three TAs had informed her they thought Ian's suggestion was not right for the school, stating it would not be well received by the long-standing community members. Further, some staff could see no real reason for the change, especially as the school achieved good results in Key Stage 2 SATs and only had 'a few Black children'. Some staff had suggested Ian's idea was 'taking political correctness too far'. These staff members had not spoken directly to Ian as they did not have the confidence to approach him openly, but had asked the Key Stage 1 leader to act as their spokesperson and protect their anonymity.

Reflective questions

1. What choices does Ian have at this time?
2. How should Ian manage this situation?
3. What steps have you taken in your organisation to implement equality legislation?

Q **Discussion: Leading a new initiative**

This is a very challenging situation. Ian has chosen to introduce an idea which has strong moral purpose and is certainly consistent with equality legislation and the need to promote equality between different groups. However, Ian now knows his idea is not popular with a sizeable proportion of the staff. Ian is the headteacher and needs to show leadership. He can choose to introduce his idea without listening to the views of his staff, which may be problematic and could make him appear belligerent; or he could reconsider and not proceed, which may make him look ineffectual. Either option presents Ian with a dilemma.

Ian seems to be working with a stable team who have experienced little change. He has used Kotter's model to an extent and tried to engage his team, including all his staff not just the senior leaders. However, before launching the idea Ian could have usefully worked to create a sense of urgency, demonstrating why this idea was needed in the school. It is of concern that his staff feel 8 per cent of the school population is only 'a few children'. Although he has experienced an initial setback, and does not currently enjoy the support of his whole team, this need not derail his plan. While Ian has secured the support of his deputy, he can now try to understand the wishes and motivations of his staff in an attempt to build a wider coalition, including other senior leaders, influential staff and the rest of the team. The idea is sound, especially in the light of changing school demographics and is consistent with the Equality Act in that it is seeking to promote relationships between different groups. The plan may still be salvaged if Ian uses the feedback he has been given to build on and modify his idea before relaunching it for September.

Implications of working ethically and achieving successful outcomes through high expectations

Children's and young people's awareness of broader society develops at different times, underpinned by their home circumstances and the wider communities they live in. Many children enter education with well-formed, and sometimes stereotypical, views and beliefs. If these views reinforce racist, homophobic or other discriminatory attitudes, education organisations need to find ways of working with young people to challenge these views to build communities which 'cater for all students' (Bossaert et al., 2013: 60) so that they are free to learn and can reach their potential.

In their research Willis and Lander found primary-school-aged children were unable to accept 'Black people [could] be British [and] … relied on skin colour to attribute characteristics to unfamiliar individuals' (2015: 36). Even though these characteristics were overwhelmingly negative, in the same research Willis and Lander also found 'racial issues were not … recognised or dealt with appropriately' (ibid.: 39) by teachers who were reluctant to take action and 'interrupt the vicious cycle of racism' (ibid.: 41). In this climate, where racism was not actively challenged, it is unlikely that minority children would be able to perform well.

In contrast when Gill and Darley, who were working as headteachers at a primary school in the north of England, found their school linked to the 7/7 bombings of 2005, they decided to address the issue directly and worked to 'relieve … tension … through the collective effort of the children, staff and parents' (Gill and Darley, 2015: 17). Gill and Darley worked hard to reverse parental perceptions of teachers' 'low expectations' (ibid.: 18) of children by reaching out to the community and developing 'teachers' understanding of the social, economic and cultural conditions [of the] community' (ibid.: 18) based on the powerful premise 'that success for one child [was] success for the whole community' (ibid.: 20). Gill and Darley's proactive stance and belief in change through positive action helped to change their school and shaped an atmosphere where children were able to learn, families felt included and everyone had a meaningful role to play in the success of school and the community.

Creating a truly inclusive learning environment built on 'respect, care, recognition and empathy' (Obiakor et al, 2012: 478) demands ensuring the well-being of all community members within a morally justified framework through 'leadership and management, high quality teaching, and strong ethos with high expectations' (Gunter, 2006: 62). It requires every member of the community to demonstrate 'mutual caring and mutual expectations [in order] to contribute to the betterment' (Fullan, 2006: 51) of the setting. Leaders must provide clear direction and show that 'ethnocentrism, that is the judging of other cultures from our own cultural perspective' (Dimmock and Walker, 2005: 9) is unacceptable.

Inclusive learning cultures act as a catalyst for change, impacting on the immediate environment and the community 'beyond the school gates' (Dyson, 2006: 117) with successful leadership, as Gill and Darley demonstrated, having the potential to produce 'positive long-term effects for … society as a whole' (Bossaert et al., 2013: 60). Through purposeful action, significant changes can be achieved where children and young people can achieve in a climate of 'mutual respect' (Gill and Darley, 2015: 20).

⍰ Reflective questions

1. What ethical challenges have you encountered in your role as an education leader?
2. What actions have you taken to manage these challenges?

◯ Discussion: Creating strong learning communities

Each situation and each environment is different. How leaders choose to manage individual cases is a matter of choice. However, the shrewd leader will gather as much information as possible to inform decision making because 'inclusion works well when all stakeholders collaborate and consult with each other' (Obiakor et al., 2012: 479). Further, the bold leader will be prepared to take risks and try something original, even in the face of challenge, if they are committed to the ideological soundness of the proposal.

Education leaders need to understand the communities they serve so that they can ensure all learners are included. While asking staff and students to think and behave differently may initially be difficult, it is necessary to enable 'opportunities to be accessed and realized' (Knowles and Lander, 2011: 13). Without clear leadership, children and young people may be left to the idiosyncrasies of individual teachers and without a champion to support their progression. Success of learning communities can only be ensured when all members of the community agree to work together for the overall benefit of that community, putting any individual disagreements aside. This takes time, and energy 'needs to be invested in ensuring that partnerships develop and have an impact upon pupils' engagement and achievement' (Gill and Darley, 2015: 20).

In building successful communities where students can achieve, education leaders need to navigate cultural differences and:

1. Have high expectations of their students and believe all students are capable of academic success;
2. Communicate clearly … [and] involve [communities] in decision making;
3. Use culturally relevant teaching approaches;
4. Use … teaching strategies that promote coherence, relevance, progression and continuity.

(Adapted from Obiakor et al., 2012: 487)

Only through the help and support of a strong coalition can leaders hope to successfully introduce and implement lasting change for the benefit of the entire community.

Summary

In this chapter we have explored the ethical challenges for leaders of promoting inclusion in education and ensuring compliance with recent equality legislation. Leaders operate in a rigorous externally audited environment where they must demonstrate to multiple individuals and organisations the success of their decisions. Government agencies and families want evidence that leaders have driven organisations forward, transforming the organisation to provide better outcomes for learners through the resourceful deployment of staff. Education-specific Acts such as Every Child Matters (2003) and generic national legislation including the Equality Act (2010) and the statutory Special Educational Needs and Disability Code of Practice (2015), have established a framework which embeds fairness into the daily responsibilities of education leaders. While there is now a legal imperative to ensure equality and inclusion in education, this will not be easily achieved in all organisations and leaders will need to develop a compelling argument for change and a strategic plan for implementation to support introduction, development and maintenance of inclusive practice.

Lewin claimed 'there is nothing so practical as a good theory' (1952: 169) and when implementing change leaders need to make good use of recognised theoretical frameworks, such as Kotter's eight-step and Lewin's three-step models, to guide their actions.

References

Bossaert, G., Colpin, H., Pijl, S. J. and Petry, K. (2013) Truly included? A literature study focussing on the social dimension of inclusion in education. *International Journal of Inclusive Education,* 17 (1): 60–79.

Brighouse, H., Tooley, J. and Howe, K. R. (2010) *Educational Equality.* London: Continuum.

Department for Education (DfE) (2014) *The Equality Act 2010 and Schools: Departmental Advice for School Leaders, School Staff, Governing Bodies and Local Authorities.* Available at www.gov. uk/government/uploads/system/uploads/attachment_data/file/315587/Equality_Act_Advice_ Final.pdf (accessed 12 August 2016).

Department for Education (DfE) (2015) *Special Educational Needs and Disability Code of Practice: 0 to 25 years. Statutory Guidance for Organisations which Work with and Support Children and Young People who have Special Educational Needs or Disabilities.* Available at www.gov.uk/ government/uploads/system/attachment_data/file/398815/SEND_Code_of_Practice_ January_2015.pdf (accessed 14 August 2016).

Dimmock, C. and Walker, A. (2005) *Educational Leadership: Culture and Diversity*. London: Sage.

Dyson, A. (2006) Beyond the school gates: Context, disadvantage and urban schools. In M. Ainscow and M. West (eds) *Improving Urban Schools – Leadership and Collaboration.* Maidenhead: Open University Press.

Equality and Human Rights Commission, *The Public Sector Equality Duty.* Available at www.equalityhumanrights.com/en/corporate-reporting/equality-and-diversity/public-sector-equality-duty (accessed 12 August 2016).

Fullan, M. (2003) *The Moral Imperative of School Leadership.* California and London: Corwin Press.

Fullan, M. (2006) *Turn Around Leadership.* California: Jossey Bass.

Gill, N. and Darley, H. (2015) Creating a community to be proud of? *Race Equality Teaching,* 33 (2): 17–20.

Gillborn, D. (2008) *Racism and Education – Coincidence or Conspiracy?* Abingdon: Routledge.

Gunter, H. (2006) Confounding stereotypes: Risk, resilience and achievement in urban schools. In M. Ainscow and M. West (eds) *Improving Urban Schools – Leadership and Collaboration.* Maidenhead: Open University Press.

Knowles, G. and Lander, V. (2011) *Diversity, Equality and Achievement in Education.* London: Sage.

Kotter, J. P. (1996) *Leading Change.* Boston, MA: Harvard Business School Press.

Kotter, J. (2012) *Leading Change,* revised edn. Boston, MA: HBR Books.

Lewin, K. (1952) *Field Theory in Social Science: Selected Theoretical Papers by Kurt Lewin.* London: Tavistock.

Manchester, J., Gray-Miceli, D. L., Metcalf, J. A., Paolini, C. A., Napier, A. H., Coogle, C. L. and Owens, M. G. (2014) Facilitating Lewin's change model with collaborative evaluation in promoting evidence-based practices of health professionals. *Evaluation and Planning,* 47: 82–90.

Obiakor, F.E., Harris, M., Mutia, K., Rotatori, A. and Algozzine, B. (2012) Making inclusion work in general education classrooms. *Education and Treatment of Children,* 35 (3): 477–490.

Ofsted (2010) *The Special Educational Needs and Disability Review – A Statement is Not Enough.* Available at www.gov.uk/government/uploads/system/uploads/attachment_data/file/413814/Special_education_neeeds_and_disability_review.pdf (accessed 13 August 2016).

Peart, S. (2013) *Making Education Work: How Black Boys and Men Navigate Further Education.* London: Trentham Books and the Institute of Education Press.

Peart, S. (2014) *Equality and Diversity in Further Education.* Northwich: Critical Publishing.

Riley-Smith, B. (2015) Sex education 'should be made compulsory in primary schools'. *Telegraph,* 17 February 2015. Available at http://www.telegraph.co.uk/news/politics/11416312/Sex-education-should-be-made-compulsory-in-primary-schools.html (accessed 14 August 2016).

Ruebain, D. and Peart, S. (2016) Disabled children, inclusion and the law in England and Wales. In G. Richards, G. and F. Armstrong (eds) *Key Issues for Teaching Assistants – Working in Diverse and Inclusive Classrooms.* London: Routledge.

Terzi, L. (2008) *Justice and Equality in Education – A Capability Perspective on Disability and Special Educational Needs.* London: Continuum.

Willis, G. and Lander, V. (2015) Why do the mirrors lie? *Race Equality Teaching,* 33(2): 28–31.

5 The structure of education

New frameworks and models

Chapter aims

When you have finished reading this chapter you will be able to:

1. understand how educational organisations have changed and some of the challenges they face;
2. outline the role of different multi-agency staff supporting these educational settings and what this can mean for you;
3. identify how different strategies are used by leaders in change management.

Overview of the chapter

The simple, historic models of education where Whitehall (DfE, 2014) was a distant echo and Local Authorities directly controlled schools and their budgets are now an artefact of the past. Successive British governments have worked to ostensibly decrease centralisation of power, while imposing a rigid system of inspection which has increased professional accountability at all levels. Given the dramatic changes in the educational landscape as regards to the structure of education, the focus now seems to have moved from schools working independently of each other to a more collaborative and partnership-orientated model. This means there is now less reliance on Local Authorities (LA) with a consequent growth of new frameworks and models to illustrate new ways of working. We demonstrate this through showing how different educational organisations like academies, state schools and faith schools work in such new ways. As a consequence, many are forming a wide range of professional relationships with each other, health and social services, for the success of their schools. We reflect on a few examples of multi-agency working before analysing how leaders are managing change with new, or at least, modified frameworks and educational models.

> **Key words:** academy; collaboration; leadership; multi-agency; team work.

Introduction

In England, we are seeing rapid changes in the educational landscape with the growth and development of different types of educational institutions such as academies. This has given an opportunity for the growth of autonomy for schools and the empowering of school leaders to try out new things, new curricula, take risks and be creative in offering an excellent learning experience for their learners. According to the education White Paper: Education Excellence Everywhere (DfE, 2016b), this implies leaders can create the conditions required for excellence, managed and led by a school-led system, or have a model of working totally under their control, yet accountable to outside agency, like Ofsted. This chapter starts by discussing what the different educational organisations are and how they have changed. The discussion moves on to how these changes mean different ways of working for staff to ensure that partnerships are fostered and maintained across multi-agency teams. Finally, we look at some of the challenges faced in practice through change management.

What are the different types of organisations in education?

There are many different types of organisations in education, ranging from the Early Years in terms of Sure Start centres and nurseries to primary and secondary state schools, special schools, faith schools, private schools and academies. Furthermore, these organisations include those in further and higher education. These organisations cater for education provision from Early Years to post-16 education. For example, all children in England between the ages of 5 and 16 are entitled to a free place at a state school where they have to follow the National Curriculum. In brief, the most common state schools are:

- community schools, controlled by the local council and not influenced by business or religious groups;
- foundation schools and voluntary schools, which have more freedom to change the way they do things than community schools;
- academies, run by a governing body, independent from the local council – they can follow a different curriculum;
- grammar schools, run by the council, a foundation body or a trust – they select all or most of their pupils based on academic ability and there is often an exam to get in;
- faith schools – in England these schools teach a general curriculum with a particular religious character or formal links with a religious organisation.

We have recently seen the formation of academies. Academies are publicly funded independent schools. They receive their funding directly from central government, rather than through a Local Authority. The day-to-day running of the school lies with the headteacher or principal, but they are overseen by individual charitable bodies called academy trusts and may be part of an academy chain. These trusts and chains provide advice, support, expertise and a strategic overview. All schools, primary as well as secondary, have been invited to convert to academy status, with priority being given to the best performers.

The Academies Act 2010 allowed a large number of academies to be formed from September 2010, and for the numbers to grow each year. Academies were to be funded directly by the government, rather than through Local Authorities like state-funded schools, at a comparable level to maintained schools (Academies Act, 2010). At the end of July 2015, there were 846 multi-academy trusts in England (Hill, 2015).

There is debate both for and against the benefits of academies. Some say they drive up standards by putting more power in the hands of headteachers over pay, length of the school day and term times, they have more freedom to innovate and can opt out of the National Curriculum. This area needs more research (Hill et al., 2012: 102).

How have these educational organisations changed?

As state schools, there were no formal partnerships except local ones created by a network of schools. One of the main changes now is an increase in multi-academy trusts (MATs) with formal arrangements for partnerships and collaborations involving academies. The DfE expects most schools to form or join MATs and is establishing a MAT growth fund to create new MATs and support the expansion of existing ones. There will be Regional Schools Commissioners (RSCs) formed who will encourage high-performing schools to 'extend their influence' and grow the MATs in their region. This change means that MATs will have to work hard when taking on new schools, requiring meetings to establish accountability roles and measures.

What this structural change in the education sector means is freedom and autonomy to model new ways of working like partnerships and collaborations involving different agencies and staff. As the Department for Education (DfE, 2016a) observes, 'there are a range of ways in which schools can work together as a formal partnership, from loose collaborations with no shared governance to being part of the same multi-academy trust'. This collaborative, multi-agency approach is explored in the next section.

Multi-agency working – roles and responsibilities

The role of LAs has changed dramatically since 2000, as described earlier, and currently they have limited relationships with schools, thus necessitating innovative ways of working with new structures, policies and models of practice. Public services are now delivered through intricate collaborations and partnerships working together to achieve positive outcomes for young learners and their families. For example, Susan is an operations manager responsible for Young People's Services. She leads 'Safework', which is a specialist organisation in the county providing supported housing and related services to homeless and vulnerable people, which requires collaboration with different agencies. She is responsible for ensuring that all services in her group are well coordinated, the accommodation is of a high standard, and health and safety is adhered to. Susan ensures this is achieved through group meetings, individual supervisions with service managers, and smaller focus groups when needed. The example above shows that organisations are having to work differently now with and across different agencies and people, through multi-agency working. By multi-agency working we mean bringing together professionals from similar backgrounds that could be integrated to provide a more effective system to meet individual needs. For example, within education this workforce would include health workers, teachers, support staff and social services employees.

Fitzgerald and Kay (2008) consider multi-agency working to involve more than one agency working with a child and/or parents, however this does not always mean working together. There are other approaches including intra-professional working (this is a team of professionals who are all from the same profession, such as three physical therapists collaborating on the same case), inter-professional (this refers to the working relationships between different groups of professionals, for example between social workers, teachers and police officers) and inter-agency (here, consideration must be given to the collaboration between organisations rather than the professionals within them – for example, looking at the Local Authority adult and community services rather than the social worker), involving different levels of integration and collaboration between team members. The focus of inter-agency working is on the child and their family when planning and assessing provision.

It is this inter-dependency, this interconnectedness, which is creating the contemporary challenge in academies. This is not tried and tested ground, as 'we have not been here before' (Linsky and Lawrence, 2011: 12).

Multi agency working – what does this mean in practice?

McKimm (2009) highlights that the '2020 Children and Young People's Workforce strategy' has set out the government's vision and values for how integrated practice can work effectively in order to resolve any issues. These aspirations state that every childcare worker should be:

- excellent in their practice;
- have ambitions for every child and young person;
- be committed to partnership and integrated working;
- be respected and valued as a professional.

As part of these integrated services, multi-agency teams are set up as a more formal arrangement to share common goals and they tend to be managed by one member of the team. Tighter systems regarding sharing information within these teams have been implemented since significant flaws were identified within child protection services following the tragic death of Victoria Climbié in 2000 and Baby P in 2007. They work together in practice by having clear roles and responsibilities and clear lines of communication in their interactions.

We believe authentic leadership can be adapted to meet the needs of stakeholders in delivering integrated children services. The role of, for example, arranging timely meetings between a headteacher, a family and a social worker, requires of the social worker, as a multi-agency agent, good management skills of organising and scheduling meetings, communicating the agenda to all and minute taking. The role calls for the social worker to bring all parties together by demonstrating ethical, trust and commitment values. The concern here is to lead with her heart as well as her head and thus establish long-term, meaningful relationships while maintaining self-discipline to achieve targets. At the core of this collaborative experience is that the participants strive for consistency between espoused practice and practice in action. There will be self-doubt and frustration as well as supported hope, trust and joy. So in multi-agency working, we can see insights into different people's ways of working as well as the dilemma participants face in developing new ways of working (Morrison and Arthur, 2013). One dilemma many multi-agency partnerships come across on many occasions is 'barriers' – to communication, developing trust, relationship building etc., and how to coordinate services effectively enough to break those barriers down.

Case study 5.1: Multi-agency working across Early Years in general

Priti works in an Early Years setting that has a Sure Start setting attached to a primary school in City A, and this is her story. City A has high levels of child poverty which is not too dissimilar to some of the high deprivations seen in major cities in England. Neighbouring families and their children are encouraged to access the facilities, whose intention is to improve the children's well-being as well as raising standards in education. The selection of services offered include parenting advice, breast-feeding workshops, interactive play sessions, visits from health visitors and the school nurse. All sessions have a high emphasis on promoting a healthy lifestyle and raising aspirations within vulnerable families. This inter-agency umbrella, which encompasses the health sector, play, childcare provision, social care, police and youth support, is an ambitious innovation, bringing influences which can have massive impact on childcare and development.

One of Priti's responsibilities is to liaise with staff when the need arises, including speech therapists, the school nurse, the autism advisory team and staff from our on-site

Sure Start children's centre. Many outside agencies influence the teaching and support given within my role as a Foundation 1 teaching assistant, but as I provide lesson plans and input for our youngest set of children, it is the Children's Centre teacher that I liaise with the most frequently. Subsequently, I focused primarily on the inter-professionalism developed between our Early Years unit and this multi-agency professional.

To gain a clearer perspective on multi-agency working, I conducted an interview with the Children's Centre teacher employed on-site, and an additional Children's Centre teacher employed by County Council A. Three issues that I felt were most prominently highlighted as barriers to effective, collaborative working were:

1. communication;
2. training;
3. working as a partnership/team.

1. Communication

The analysis with reference to the multi-agency work of the Children's Centre's teacher on-site clearly stated that a potential barrier to effective team work was that important information was often withheld. It transpired that the reason for this was that staff often get possessive about children in their settings. During our interview she iterated that she did not feel this was true to our setting as the team freely communicated and felt it essential to support each other; by being open about any issues or concerns either of us had regarding individual families. We mutually run a 'Ready, Steady, Go' group that allows children and their families to meet during six play sessions prior to them starting their education in Early Years. She commented that these were highly effective sessions, allowing the key worker to introduce themselves andeasing the transition into formal education. She also stated this group was invaluable to identify any needs for intervention, for example speech and language therapy or any concerns about Special Educational Needs, allowing better target setting.

2. Training

Both Children's Centre teachers commented that one of their strengths was to provide training courses to support school across all areas of the Early Years Foundation Stage curriculum, as they have expertise in different fields. This is true of our on-site Children's Centre teacher in that she has a wide breadth of knowledge in social care policies and in using the Common Assessment Framework. Her support in offering advice to our families in need to use such agencies has been invaluable.

On a personal level, the Children's Centre teacher employed by County A is also an Early Years specialist teacher. She provides training on behavioural management strategies in Early Years. Currently, I have a particularly troubled child within my key group, with environmental factors affecting his behaviour both inside and outside of school. We were able to devise an intervention programme suitable for his current needs that included time out boxes, dough to ease frustration, and happy/sad faces for him to express his mood on each particular day. These strategies enabled us to be more inclusive at group times but also laid out clear boundaries that he had to comply with, and rules that he understood were non-negotiable. For example, throwing toys, climbing on children, and shouting through inputs were all behaviours that were unacceptable. The rules were consistent and known across all staff members. Through parental liaison it transpired that rules and boundaries were clearly lacking from his home life. A clear example is illustrated here where multi-agency working can help improve a child's access to education.

3. Working as a partnership/team

There was high need to ensure that information is passed on to the correct team member within the Early Years unit. Between myself, the Children's Centre teacher and my job-share partner this is essential to provide consistency for the children to keep track of their learning. For example, lesson plans for teaching will be different at the beginning of the week, covering different elements of the Early Years Foundation Stage. Assessment sheets and modes of recording, i.e. sticky notes, photographic evidence and narrative observations taken from each input, need to be shared between both job-share partners. This will ensure that achievement and attainment can be tracked successfully, without any gaps in their learning.

Within the Foundation 1 team, I feel that this is a current weakness, partially due to personality differences. As part of a job-share arrangement, I feel my partner prefers to take control and take credit for actions not always entirely of her own doing. Consequently, I feel that the partnership is becoming more competitive, rather than complementary.

Q **Discussion: Education support workers**

Findings from Case study 5.1 illustrate the importance of educational support workers having a basic knowledge and understanding of each individual's role. The rationale is that agencies should complement, not compete against each other. The goal is to ultimately provide better all-round care and educational support, tailored to individual families.

To overcome the disadvantaged area highlighted in Case study 5.1, all practitioners involved should critically reflect on their work ethics and evaluate frequently. One way to achieve this is to improve lines of communication across agencies, through regular meetings, email communications, video-conferencing and group-chat forums, and also by constantly updating knowledge and skills through regular training courses. It is essential that practitioners should keep abreast of local and national policies that impact on their work with children and families. Foley (2008: 279) states that all practitioners involved in work with children should consider that any development of skills, knowledge and values needs to be 'rooted in the realities and issues within children's lives' and keeping empathy at the forefront every time.

The 2020 Children and Young People's Workforce Strategy sets out the government's vision and values that everyone who works with children and young people should be 'committed to partnership and integrated working' (DCSF, 2008: 6–7). According to McKimm and Phillips (2009: ix), at the moment we have a 'siloed provision' of agencies, inferring separate ways of working. We need an alignment of greater integration and collaboration across boundaries. This implies the need for sharper leadership competencies and skills to work across traditional boundaries through building new coalitions and challenging the causes of inertia (Carter and Sood, 2014).

Working with multi-agency colleagues requires from leaders a number of skills and competences. Scott et al. (2012) identify the need for political awareness, risk-taking ability, greater awareness of safeguarding issues and better working relationships with elected members. The leadership challenge here is to ensure sensitive and common use of language when speaking across boundaries (Scott et al., 2012).

Case study 5.2: Multi-agency working across the Local Authority

This case study is about a multi-agency worker called Jo. She is a member of the Joint Access Teams (JATs) within a (named) county who is currently leading on the review of the JATs for Children's Services. Jo's role requires her to work collaboratively while acknowledging the contribution JATs have made to building confidence. Jo has the responsibility to clearly evidence how JATs have contributed to improving outcomes in families. She also has to work on enhancing safeguarding at a local level and ensuring safeguarding is 'everyone's business'. In all these activities, Jo maintains existing partnerships and is developing improved partnerships particularly with GPs, district councils and social care. In terms of accountability, Jo ensures everyone is clear who the JAT is accountable to. Jo's role is to work with partners and the senior leadership to further analyse priorities, opportunities and challenges set out in Table 5.1, being mindful of the issues of managing within an environment of challenge and complexity.

Table 5.1 Opportunities and challenges

Opportunities	Challenges
• JATs have a key role to play in contributing to appropriate referrals to Children's Social Care and to continue to work with families that do not meet the Children's Social Care threshold. • CAF, Team Around the Child and Team Around the Family (TAC and TAF) are well supported by JATs. JAT members often support colleagues new to these processes and establishing CAF meetings. • The JAT meetings provide a key opportunity to hold services to account to ensure that actions are allocated to personnel within services and followed up robustly. • The added value provided by JATs ensures that key agencies are involved together at an early help stage to respond to families' needs. • JATs provide an opportunity to enhance safeguarding at a local level by monitoring cases at level 3 on the Pathway to Provision and taking a collective view regarding referral to social care at level 4 if needed. • Parents are supported to attend JATs. Parents report that they welcome the opportunity to be listened to and see that professionals are going to support them in a coordinated way.	• Many services have reduced staff and reconfigured in recent times, which impacts on JAT membership. JATs are particularly noticing a gap with social care and CAMHS representation. • Some JAT professionals have expressed concern about the challenge of gaining consent from resistant families. • There is a need for more clarity about how the JAT fits with the 'Early Help Offer' within County Council X. • There are ongoing issues relating to cross-border work with other authorities, although the JATs can provide opportunities to resolve these on a local level for individual families. • JAT referrals have reduced as the workforce is better informed about service provision – how do we ensure value for money in light of the falling number of cases? • Need to clarify the role of JAT in relation to other multi-agency networks at a local level. • Need to ensure the role that JATs perform in terms of enhancing safeguarding at a local level is not lost.

A changed working regime means Jo involves parents and carers in a meaningful way. One major ongoing challenge is resources, in terms of capacity within reduced staff teams to contribute to JATs. This is summarised in Table 5.2.

Table 5.2 Joint Access Teams: A partnership approach to Early Help

Workforce	Acknowledging the contribution JATs have made to building confidence within the workforce regarding integrated working.
Impact	Being able to clearly evidence how JATs have contributed to improving outcomes in families.
Safeguarding	Enhancing safeguarding at a local level and ensuring safeguarding is 'everyone's business'.
Partnerships	Maintaining existing good partnerships and developing improved partnerships particularly with GPs, district councils and social care.
Accountability	Ensuring everyone is clear who the JAT is accountable to.
Participation	Ensuring the involvement of parents and carers is meaningful.
Resources	Ongoing challenge regarding capacity within reduced staff teams to contribute to JATs.

Q Discussion: Example of change management

Jo brought about one change in her organisation – developing a dynamic team that collaborated together for the same outcomes for children and families. She used her persuasive and diplomatic skills to bring about change (see change management ideas in other chapters in this book). In essence, change meant using a range of leadership and management knowledge, skills and attributes to understand what the problem was and how to resolve it with positive outcomes by working as a team to address it. Jo knew that she had to explain why changes were needed, so ensured there was a focus on results and outcomes. What she did was to use her ability to create and sustain commitment across a system, thus aligning people to work towards a common goal. She knew that to succeed they needed to work collaboratively. What Jo actually did was to lead through influence rather than power while always maintaining a common and shared vision for children's services. She demonstrated a belief in her team and people – fostering a sense of team and team practices that enabled working through others. She attained her goal of collaborative working through leading by example, believing in others and encouraging professionals from across different backgrounds. This had an impact on the team and the families and children they worked with, by meeting their needs quicker, reducing paperwork and having more open communication. These changes were successful because Jo and her team were:

1. focusing on results and outcomes;
2. ensuring that the improvement of outcomes was the overarching priority;
3. remaining accountable but for results not the process;
4. collaborating together;
5. creating and sustaining commitment across a system – aligning people to work towards a common goal;
6. demonstrating a belief in people;
7. creating a climate in which people can learn, i.e. a safe one where mistakes can be made;
8. demonstrating the ability to see things through and work through challenges;
9. removing unnecessary complexity from systems, and also in creating a simple, clear narrative or strategy;
10. trying new tools and techniques and adapting them as necessary.

(Adapted from Coleman and Glover, 2010)

Managing complexity in an integrated services agenda requires the need for new frameworks and models. Given the opportunities and challenges outlined above with regard to JAT development and Jo's role and responsibilities, there are several leadership implications. Collaborative leadership is the key to driving JAT development. However, we need to be aware of the issues of managing within an environment of challenge and complexity.

Managing complex environments

McKimm and Phillips (2009: 141) identify three guiding principles for leaders working in partnerships who are managing in complex environments (see Table 5.3).

We now turn to looking at a few of the advantages and disadvantages of multi-agency working (see Table 5.4).

In Table 5.4, it is important to understand that child and family care comes first and that the educational experience of the learner is made least disruptive in a child protection issue. The 1989 Children's Act (DfE, 2015) is statutory involving inter-agency

Table 5.3 Guiding principles and leadership in partnerships

Guiding principles – Leadership in partnerships
1. Individuals need to know themselves, be emotionally intelligent in their relationships with others and deploy behaviours that fit the context.
2. Individuals and organisations must be able to relate to other partners/stakeholders, be vulnerable to influence and receptive to complementary forms of leadership
3. Uncertainty and unintended consequences often result from interventions into complex systems. Organisations and partnerships therefore need to have faith in self-regulation and acknowledge the limits of policy-led regulation and political leadership.

Table 5.4 Advantages and disadvantages of multi-agency working

Advantages	*Disadvantages*
Child at the centre means whole picture to be seen	Resource intensive
Child and family involved in discussion	If allocated a non-dedicated person to the child and family
Cuts down on paperwork	Retelling the same thing to different people
People attend fewer meetings so less time is needed and joint meetings mean joint aims, objectives and advice or action can be taken (Atkinson et al., 2007)	Multiple meetings and possibly different agendas
Quicker access to services and earlier identification and intervention which in the long term will save resources (Atkinson et al., 2007)	Time consuming and late decision-making changes (Collins and McCray, 2012)
Gaps in provision can easily be seen and rectified by a multi-agency approach (Collins and McCray, 2012)	Gaps missed due to delays
Multi-agency working enhances the understanding of the family as a whole and deepens the awareness of each individual situation (Sure Start, 2000)	May cause confusion with different people seen and each agency has different views on who should know what so this could hamper the holistic approach (ethical issues)

collaboration and joint working. This offers many opportunities and challenges for a wide variety of multi-agency teams working in different contexts and different settings like state schools and academies. State-funded schools provide education to pupils between the ages of 3 and 18 without charge and funded through national and local taxes. Academy schools were formed in 1997 to replace poorly performing schools in areas of high social and economic deprivation.

However, what is unclear going forward is how to address differing professional principles, attitudes to sharing information, the terminology used by different professionals, funding arguments, and lack of clarity in roles and responsibilities (Brown and White, 2006). There are many areas of good practice and ways to improve practice according to Atkinson et al. (2007), such as trust and respect for all members of the team, regular joint planning meetings, joint funding and resource sharing, as well as a clear work focus and joint ownership. The main focus for all multi-agency work should be the well-being of the learners/young people and their family.

Q Discussion: Multi-agency working

One difficulty in multi-agency working is assessing the success criteria of a team. Different agencies measure performance differently. For example, social workers are often assessed on caseload, meaning they may be at a disadvantage in their service when working in a team looking at early intervention where families are not entered on the social services database due to support being preventative rather than statutory (Moran et al., 2006). This often leads to quantity of time rather than quality of action being the measure of performance. The example above shows the need for accurate record keeping of meetings and ensuring any action is carefully discussed by the case worker in collaboration with the family.

Let us turn to a case study of a teaching assistant (called Julie) working as part of a team in her secondary school with a social worker.

Case study 5.3: Multi-agency working across different schools

The case involved a family of four children who attended two different schools and a nursery, with the added complication of a parent being in prison so their legal representative was always present.

The team consisted initially of a social worker, health visitor (for the youngest child) and school nurse (for the eldest three), educational psychologist, education welfare officer, headteacher from primary school and nursery, child protection officer from secondary school, community paediatrician and Julie (teaching assistant) as well as the mother with her legal representative and the father's legal representative.

The team had been put together to specifically investigate the child protection issue and monitor the progress of the child or children involved. The individuals had never worked together before the team was drawn up and there was no element of choice about becoming a team member. According to Tuckman (1965), groups go through stages of development 'forming, storming, norming and performing', but this team needed to become a functioning unit immediately due to the serious nature of the issue.

Due to the similar specialisms within this team but for different children within the family, Julie felt it was hard to divide power and therefore the team started off really being individuals working with the same family, which supports the findings of Simkins and Garrick (2012) on the reality of some multi-agency teams.

Julie was part of each team because she was the learner's key worker within her school which meant she saw the learner daily. Therefore, she had a good working relationship with the learner and regular contact with home. Julie was able to see how they were being affected by their situation. However, she had no previous experience of working within a multi-disciplinary team. In this situation Julie felt she had least experience of multi-agency working which made her feel vulnerable. Often it meant she had more work to carry out as Julie had no-one to pass her concerns to.

☐ Discussion: Julie's dilemma

In Case study 5.3, the dilemma faced by Julie is clear. The tasks she had were often difficult as she had no authority within the school to access any funding and she often ended up doing the task with no support. Some of the tasks were not part of her role and special permission from school, parents and health care workers was needed to carry out these tasks, requiring sensitive handling. Although these tasks were not part of her official role, she carried them out as she knew the safety and well-being of the child was at stake. This situation required a good working relationship with the family and the social worker, where the role of Julie was seen as a key catalyst.

Change management – bringing it together

There have been huge changes to the structure of education generally as well as multi-agency working that we discussed earlier. McKimm and Phillips consider the field of integrated work in health, social care and others to have become even more complex with the involvement of 'multiple agencies, professionals and other stakeholders' (2009: ix). The immediate challenge appears to be that of managing disparate systems and structures and considering how best to integrate some of the differences and dilemmas born of such a range of professionals. They call for the 'urgent need for collaborative leaders and managers' (ibid.) to build new alliances and work across traditional boundaries. These new leaders will require energy and emotional intelligence to challenge disputes and causes of inertia.

Managing change with a different range of staff in different school settings is not only difficult, but very demanding on leadership skills, competencies and experiences. Most school settings will have developed different policies and processes reflecting their own context. This may be a broad framework of approaches that use some tried-and-tested processes. Whatever the model, it has to improve practice. Bell and Stevenson's (2006: 13) model of policy into practice shows that policy formation involves an awareness of the socio-political environment and plans for appropriate strategies. This requires good understanding of organisational principles and operational practices and procedures, i.e. structures and systems. However, most leaders will know that policy development does not happen in a vacuum – it requires critical debate among different stakeholders, of the school's values, mission and historical setting. Also, a 'policy impacts differently on different social groups' (Bell and Stevenson, 2006: 8).

We found that leaders of different types of educational settings used different models of change management to suit their own contexts and circumstances. A number of notable key levers in the school improvement practice noted in the literature are:

1. a clear vision for school improvement;
2. a strong emphasis on behaviour, discipline and attendance;
3. a tight grip on target setting, pupil tracking and performance monitoring, linked to raising pupils' aspirations and expectations;
4. ensuring curriculum content is relevant to student ability;
5. the intensive use of formative assessment to provide feedback to students;
6. intensive support for student in exam years, for example, Year 11;
7. building up the capacity of teachers to deliver high-quality lessons through feedback via frequent lesson observations and programmes such as the improving and outstanding teacher programmes;
8. developing and coaching middle and senior leaders;
9. practising action research among staff from different schools in the chain;
10. working with and securing the support of parents.

(Hill et al., 2012: 66)

Activity: Change management

In your school, what is the policy and practice for something that is in the process of being changed, for example, sorting out behaviour, discipline and attendance?

Q **Discussion: Complexity of change management**

By reflecting on this activity, you will understand the complexity of change management. The need to communicate with different people to ensure everyone has the same understanding of the issue then becomes important. Getting feedback from people is also vital as it ensures ownership and a form of commitment to the change issue. What has been your experience of being involved in change activity? What were the tensions and stress points, and how did you deal with these? People naturally resist change (Armstrong, 2009). Beer et al. (1990) offer a number of strategies to minimise tension and stress, such as make a commitment to change, identify who will do what tasks, get others involved through demonstrating personal energies, check progress of self and others and make necessary adjustments if problems arise, do this collectively.

An effective education system in England is dependent on good leadership and supportive teams created by identifying and maximising individual's skills and knowledge to undertake roles (Morrison, 2013) – this is necessary for improving standards. Some of the causes of change failure include not being clear about the problem and using inappropriate change ideas due to the inexperience of staff or not fully understanding the cultural implications.

In putting policy into practice, here are a few ideas deployed by teaching staff working with multi-agency staff:

* Improve lines of communication across agencies.
* Constantly update knowledge and skills through regular training courses.
* Keep abreast of local and national policies that impact on your work with children and families.
* For all practitioners involved in work with children, consider that any development of skills, knowledge and values needs to be 'rooted in the realities and issues within children's lives' (Collins and Foley, 2008: 279).
* Keep empathy at the forefront every time.

Reflecting on the work of Lumby and Coleman (2016: 182–184), here are some possible goals and actions for change management. Context matters, so plan action that meets everyone's needs and not just those of selective groups, thus increasing equality. Look at the outcomes for learners as well as the process that informs it. Persistent action in the long term leads to change, so do it collectively. Look at the structures, policies and procedures, stand back, reflect, offer new alternatives and a range of solutions for your school context, and do not assume it is someone else's fault or responsibility. We need to support each other to bring about change and not let deficit be the focus – and as Lumby and Coleman (2016: 184), say, 'keep going'.

Summary

In conclusion we have explored the different challenges faced in providing high-quality education in different types of school settings in England. The role and engagement of teaching and support staff with multi-agency staff in different school settings was discussed. This recognised the need for effective communication, team work and trust in promoting collaborative partnership as professionals. We identified strategies and styles leaders used in different settings with a different range of staff to ensure the policy and procedures involved were successful. We have encouraged you to develop an informed critical approach and self-reflection that pools your professional commitment to providing high-quality education with a healthy cynicism of working with new, or at least, modified frameworks and educational models.

Reflecting on the case studies and literature, a number of principles emerge for consideration. Firstly, leadership is about a vision, a passion to make a difference, a better future for the community, better delivered as a shared, collaborative, distributed venture. This means letting go of the past and looking at new ways to solve problems based on leaders having a moral compass. Secondly, forming new academies, trusts and other organisations offers one approach to leading and managing change, but there are many more, requiring fitness for purpose and this may require using multiple lenses to achieve resolution. Thirdly, leaders need to accept responsibility for their actions, but to do this through empowering others for multiple leadership roles. The final principle is that leadership is an ongoing journey and risk taking and creativity offer major challenges to achieve the desired vision.

References

Academies Act (2010) An Act to make provision about academies. http://www.legislation.gov.uk/ukpga/2010/32/contents (accessed 25 October 2016).

Armstrong, M. (2009) *Armstrong's Handbook of Management and Leadership – A Guide to Managing for Results*, 2nd edn. London: Kogan Page.

Atkinson, M., Jones, M. and Lamont, E. (2007) CfBT Literature Review: *Multi-Agency Working and its Implications for Practice.* http://www.nfer.ac.uk/publications/MAD01/MAD01.pdf (accessed 2 September 2016).

Beer, M., Eisenstat, R. and Spector, B. (1990) Why change programs don't produce change. *Harvard Business Review,* November–December: 158–166.

Bell, L. and Stevenson, H. (2006) Citizenship and social justice: Developing education policy in multi-ethnic schools. In *Education Policy Process, Themes and Impact*. Abingdon: Routledge.

Brown, K. and White, K. (2006) *Exploring the Evidence Base for Integrated Children's Services.* Available at http://www.scotland.gov.uk/Publications/2006/01/24120649/0 (accessed 31 August 2016).

Carter, K. and Sood, K. (2014) It's complicated: apprentice leaders on the edge of chaos. *Management in Education*, 28 (2): 64–69.

Coleman, M. and Glover, D. (2010) *Educational Leadership and Management: Developing Insights and Skills*. Maidenhead: Open University Press and McGraw-Hill Education.

Collins, J. and Foley, P. (2008) *Promoting Children's Wellbeing: Policy and Practice*. Bristol: Policy Press and the Open University.

Collins, F. and McCray, J. (2012) Partnership working in services for children: Use of the common assessment framework. *Journal of Interprofessional Care,* 26: 134–140.

Department for Children, Schools and Families (DCSF) (2008) *Building Brighter Futures: Next Steps for the Children's Workforce*. Nottingham: DCSF. Available at www.teachernet.gov.uk (accessed 3 June 2011).

Department for Education (DfE) (2014) *Collection – Schools: Statutory Guidance*. https://www.gov.uk/government/collections/statutory-guidance-schools (accessed 10 November 2015).

Department for Education (DfE) (2015) *The Children Act 1989 Guidance and Regulations Volume 2: Care Planning, Placement and Case Review*. https://www.gov.uk/government/uploads/system/uploads/attachment_data/file/441643/Children_Act_Guidance_2015.pdf (accessed 14 December 2015).

Department for Education (DfE) (2016a) *Convert to an Academy: Guide for Schools*. https://www.gov.uk/guidance/convert-to-an-academy-information-for-schools/1-before-you-apply (accessed 10 September 2016).

Department for Education (DfE) (2016b) *Educational Excellence Everywhere*. https://www.gov.uk/government/...data/.../Educational_Excellence_Everywhere (accessed 3 September 2016).

Fitzgerald, D. and Kay, J. (2008) *Working Together in Children's Services*. Abingdon: Routledge.

Foley, P. (2008) Reflecting on skills for work with children. In P. Foley and A. Rixon (eds) *Changing Children's Services: Working and Learning Together*. Milton Keynes: Policy Press, pp. 269–279.

Hill, R. (2015) The rise and rise of multi-academy trusts – latest DfE data. Available at https://roberthilleducationblog.com/2015/08/31/the-rise-and-rise-of-multi-academy-trusts-latest-dfe-data/ (accessed 2 September 2016).

Hill, R., Dunford, L., Parish, N., Rea, S. and Sandals, L. (2012) *The Growth of Academy Chains: Implications for Leaders and Leadership*. Nottingham: National College for School Leadership.

Linsky, M. and Lawrence, J. (2011) Adaptive challenges for school leadership. In H. O'Sullivan, H. and J. West-Burnham (eds) *Leading and Managing Schools*. London: Sage, pp. 3–15.

Lumby, J. and Coleman, M. (2016) *Leading for Equality: Making Schools Fairer.* London: Sage.

McKimm, J. (2009) Professional roles and workforce development. In J. Mckimm and K. Phillips (eds) *Leadership and Management in Integrated Services*. Exeter: Learning Matters, pp. 122–140.

McKimm, J. and Phillips, K. (eds) (2009) *Leadership and Management in Integrated Services*. Exeter: Learning Matters.

Moran, P., Jacobs, C., Bunn, A. and Bifulco, A. (2007) Multi-agency working: Implications for early intervention social work team. *Child and Family Social Work*, 12: 143–151.

Morrison, A. (2013). Educational leadership and change: Structural challenges in the implementation of a shifting paradigm. *School Leadership & Management*, 33: 412–424.

Morrison, M. and Arthur, L. (2013) Leadership for inter-service practice: Collaborative leadership lost in translation? An exploration. *Educational Management and Leadership,* 41(2): 179–198.

Scott, P., Harris, J. and Florek, A. (2012) *Systems Leadership for Effective Services*. Virtual Staff College Leadership Provision for Directors of Children's Services. Nottingham: The Virtual Staff College. Available at www.virtualstaffcollege.co.uk (accessed 12 January 2013).

Simkins, T. and Garrick, R. (2012) Developing multi-agency teams: Implications of a national programme evaluation. *Management in Education,* 26 (1): 13–19.

Sure Start (2000) *Providing Good Quality Childcare and Early Learning Experiences through Sure Start.* London: DfEE.

Tuckman, B. (1965) *Four (Five) Stages of Team Development.* University of Washington. Available at http://depts.washington.edu/oei/resources/changeModels/mc_team_development.pdf (accessed 31 August 2016).

Wikipedia (2016) State funded schools: https://en.wikipedia.org/wiki/State-funded_schools_ (England) (accessed 23 September 2016). (For a more detailed explanation of the nature of types of school in the UK refer to www.gov.uk/types-of-school/overview [accessed 24 October 2016]).

6 Quality assurance

Responsibilities, liabilities and consequences

Chapter aims

When you have finished reading this chapter you will be able to:

1. demonstrate a basic understanding of the concept of quality assurance in education;
2. analyse how one school manages quality through quality process;
3. identify teachers' rights, responsibilities and legal liabilities;
4. state how leaders and practitioners play a role in bringing policies and procedures together.

Overview of the chapter

Any modern organisation has at its heart the notion of accountability for its policy goals and quality assurance processes, and explicit to this process is how an organisation promotes these policies in the way it works. In keeping with policy direction, the stakeholders in an organisation have to recognise their roles and responsibilities, and central to this in an educational setting is the promotion of high-quality teaching and learning for greatest learner achievement. With so many regular updates on educational reforms, teachers and leaders are bombarded with the task of rewriting policies and procedures, leading to greater pressure and some tensions on leaders. A quality assurance process requires attention to detail. This process needs managing with accurate data for analysis and action. It seems that the penalty one has to pay for 'greater autonomy for schools comes with the increased accountability for performance' (Cotterill, 2016: 142). Therefore, the challenge explored in this chapter is how to manage such data for accountability and how to do this as a collegial activity, requiring a break from the neatly compartmentalised boxes of working often seen in schools. The argument advanced is that the silo mentality of working does not work, for this requires a greater distribution of the range of knowledge and skills across individuals and teams.

> **Key words:** accountability; leadership; quality assurance; teams.

Introduction

This chapter starts by discussing the term quality assurance (QA) as a measure of accountability when applied to educational settings in England. All organisations need to have policies in place legally so that they can be monitored and inspected by external agents like Ofsted (House of Commons Children, Schools and Families Committee, 2009). In the simplest terms, educational organisations and practitioners need data as evidence to measure the effectiveness of our work, such as how well we are teaching or how we evaluate our learners' experience. By evaluating and analysing such data, we aim to improve. This process means your team and you are involved in the process of QA and evaluation which leads to improving the quality of your work and role.

Working alone is no longer an option. The QA process requires collaboration and whole-school distributed actions so that all are leading provision with consistency. Occasionally, the systems of 'measuring' quality are flawed at school level because they are designed by people. And people sometimes make mistakes. So at times, the system is not fit for purpose or it is 'ineffectively implemented' (Wood and Dickinson, 2011: 2) and that is what we have to work through as a team to improve matters that work for us and the learners.

This chapter addresses issues of how staff deliver quality in the classroom, and then discusses teachers' rights, responsibilities and legal liabilities. Finally, it outlines some challenges and opportunities leaders in settings address in implementing policies and procedures linked to QA.

Quality assurance – the need for accountability in education

Before moving on to defining accountability in any depth (see later in this chapter), let us explore what the QA process means in education. We define accountability as 'a minimum expectation or standard regarding the effectiveness of a particular activity' (Cotterill, 2016: 143). This means that every one of us is responsible for ensuring we deliver outcomes. In education this means the best education for our learners. In essence, if there is an issue with a product or service, the quality control part of QA should prevent it from going wrong. QA is about meeting specifications through a system designed to ensure prevention (West-Burnham, 1994: 168). It means looking carefully at how an organisation makes its policy, how it implements it and how it monitors and evaluates it – this is QA.

In order to assure quality, different people in an organisation are involved, such as teachers, leaders, governors and parents, albeit at a distance. So the leadership has to consider the following aspects of QA:

- Do we have clearly defined roles and responsibilities that we can monitor?
- Are the documents and policies to formalise procedures up to date?
- Do we have in place identification of learners' requirements?
- Is the monitoring and evaluation approach recent, relevant and clear to all?
- Are there procedures for improvement in place?

(Adapted from West-Burnham, 1994: 168)

So QA and accountability are closely related concepts as both require an evidence base, reflection and action. Case study 6.1 develops some of these points.

Case study 6.1: QA procedures in an university

Jack is an external examiner for a foundation degree course at an university in England. On an annual basis he has to report on the quality of the educational provision of this course. The purpose of the report is to enable the academic board of the university to monitor the academic standards of awards against this course. So he looks at and reports back on the quality of the course in areas such as: the quality of knowledge and skills (both general and subject specific) demonstrated by the students; the appropriateness of the overall approach to teaching, learning and assessment as indicated by student performance; the currency of the curriculum and the adequacy of learning resources (in relation to learning resources); the appropriateness of stated aims and outcomes of the course, the assessment process and the standards of student attainment against national benchmarks. This report then assists the university in making any necessary improvements to the quality of teaching and learning.

Q Discussion: The AQ process in the university

Jack found that in providing an external view to another institution's quality provision is a privileged and humbling task. The quality process described in Case study 6.1 demonstrates what the university considered to be important areas for him to comment on. Jack's feedback enables the university to continually improve its learners' experiences. This supports the university to manage its provision against its financial plans. The utilisation of the QA process is every person's responsibility so that they can audit and evidence their provision for their learners and, as West-Burnham (1994: 169) notes, follow procedures for corrective action.

Defining accountability

We look at accountability in some detail next, given it is closely allied to QA. In education we would consider the education system to be accountable for what value it is providing to service users and schools to be seen to be using the money they receive effectively (DfE, 2010). Schools are publicly funded through our taxes and are a universal state service (House of Commons Children, Schools and Families Committee, 2009). Accountability is a complicated concept, with West et al. (2011) conceptualising accountability as constituting professional, hierarchical, market, contract, legal, network and participative aspects. Each of these concepts is briefly explored in the next section.

Being an educational professional means that a teacher, leader and a teaching assistant for example behave and act professionally and carry out their teaching duties as laid out in the professional standards code (DfE, 2011). The concepts of accountability are presented in Table 6.1.

Cotterill (2016) thinks that hierarchical and market accountabilities are prominent in education policy and practice in England. For example, there is a clear hierarchical structure evident between schools and external agents, where schools are 'accountable to their local authority, DfE and Ofsted for their national test and examination results and how they spend their resources' (ibid., 144).

Such accountability must be taken seriously as poor inspection outcomes can potentially be harmful to a school's reputation, staff morale and therefore impact on home–school liaison with parents who may rightly expect accountability from a school on the quality of provision. Parents as consumers, arguably, are obliged to get all the necessary educational information from a school to make informed choices. So market accountability is important and the DfE (2010) has a clear commitment to make guidelines available for parents to make informed choices. In summary, Cotterill thinks that accountability in education is aimed at 'increasing student achievement' (2016: 145), implying all are responsible for evaluating data and disseminating it responsibly.

Table 6.1 Different types of accountability in education

Professional	These are our responsibilities as professionals, where for example, as teachers we are accountable to our learners through our teaching and learning policy implementation.
Hierarchical	Hierarchical accountability suggests reporting to a senior-ranking colleague above you, for example, a teacher reporting to a head of department or senior leader.
Market	Market accountability relates to scanning the environment of a school, for example assessing which schools parents are selecting for their children, and developing an action plan.
Contract	Contract accountability is very close to academies' hearts, for example, they are directly accountable to the Secretary of State through a contractual binding funding agreement.
Legal	Legal accountability is seen in hiring and firing staff, financial management, Special Educational Needs and health and safety, for example by headteachers and governing bodies.
Network	Here this requires listening and responding to different views of actors.
Participative	Participative accountability requires all actors to be accountable for their actions.

? **Reflective questions**

1. Who do you think your school's main accountability is to?
2. How does your school carry out the accountability process?

Q **Discussion: Accountability**

The primary responsibility of headteachers and other school leaders is to focus on securing the best possible experience of teaching and learning for learners in the classroom. This is accountability to learners, staff, parents, governors and others. This means making school-based information such as league tables and value-added measures to show where the school stands on performance more transparent and user-friendly for parents. This process is undertaken, for example, by making information about learner attainment or high expectations of behaviour and attendance clearer in the school newsletter sent home to parents.

So far we have given you an introductory understanding of the concept of QA as a measure of accountability and suggested that it is neither a straightforward concept nor is there an easy-to-fit template or framework on QA to implement. Each setting will have its own ideas to develop the QA process to best fit its context. There are frameworks for QA from Ofsted that you can explore, and there are many quality books on the market written by gurus such as Deming (philosophy of management), Crosby (concept of zero defects) and Peters (management by walking about). There may be useful ideas on QA to be developed from manufacturing industry and sources from the Department for Business, Energy and Industrial Strategy (BEIS), Department for Education (DfE), Office for Standards in Education (Ofsted), and Businessballs.

What does quality assurance mean in education?

Good teachers and effective leaders make a difference to learners' lives because they are knowledgeable and passionate about education and individual learners (O'Sullivan and West-Burnham, 2011). An outstanding teacher will know every learner in their classroom, and therefore plan their lesson, activities and assessment opportunities for successful learner outcomes in a personalised way. The teacher's role, in essence, is to plan, prepare/ organise and manage learning. Teachers are consummate professionals and promote their vision, energy, enthusiasm, love and passion for their subject and know how to make lessons fun to motivate their learners. Gathering data about learners' engagement, motivation and successes helps teachers to look at the effectiveness of their QA procedures. They can then adjust practice and procedures accordingly.

We assure quality in teaching and learning by being well organised. For example, knowing what is planned at the start and end of the lesson, doing recap activities to check an individual's understanding, knowing what knowledge and understanding is retained and applied through open-ended questions and responding to the needs of pupils with special needs. Wood and Dickinson (2011: 23) suggest that each learner may have learnt different things, but they should all have made progress towards their learning goals, an area also focused on by Ofsted inspectors. A balanced approach to learning activities that is personalised will prove that learning is occurring.

Wood and Dickinson (2011) describe how a curriculum manager observed lessons to raise the quality of teaching and learning of his staff in a college. These were the questions posed (2011: 24):

1. Is learning taking place throughout the lesson?
2. Is there a good relationship between learners and teacher that encourages participation and inclusion?
3. Is there a good level of challenge in the lesson – are all learners being pushed to achieve?
4. Are the learners actively learning?
5. Is the lesson well planned and resourced?

Case study 6.2: Setting high expectations

As head of Science, Nirala had to check that QA procedures were in place and understood by her staff to ensure there was a culture of high expectations focused on the progress and achievement of every learner. She made sure that she set aside adequate time in her busy weekly schedule to spend quality time monitoring teaching and learning and then meeting the teacher afterwards for a joint feedback meeting. Having high expectations of learners and staff was Nirala's mission for the department. She ensured that her teaching staff shared this passion with their learners by modelling high expectations of respect for all, excellent classroom behaviour, completing homework on time and other tasks. Nirala had regular team meetings to ensure that this mission was adhered to.

Q Discussion: Setting a culture of high expectations

Case study 6.2 suggests that teachers learn best when they model the departmental mission of setting high expectations of their learners. It shows that when teachers work collaboratively and are passionate about their subject, they model excellence in the classroom for their learners. A culture of high expectation is brought about by being a reflective practitioner continually developing through reading, attending courses, research and challenging each other about what is quality education (Szabo and Lambert, 2002). It seems natural then to observe that delivering quality in the classroom requires outstanding teachers, but this may be a contested argument as other qualities of teaching are as important, such as the educational context and, as Wood and Dickenson argue, 'outstanding teachers are not perfect or infallible' (2011: 14). These ideas have close association with a constructivist approach to learning, where staff learn from each other through interaction, discussion and professional dialogue (Muijs and Harris, 2006).

As leadership and learning are mutually supportive and reinforcing (Fullan, 2004), so is monitoring and evaluation for the QA process. Mujis and Harris (2006: 961) have explained that leaders have to undertake six activities to link teachers' learning and teachers' leadership as they are important aspects of QA process. These are adapted below:

- Continue to teach and to improve proficiency and skill.
- Undertake peer review of the teaching process.
- Provide curriculum development knowledge.
- Participate in school-level decision making.
- Lead in-service training and staff development activities.
- Collaborate with each other by reflecting and researching.

Let us reflect on some of these areas in Case study 6.3.

Case study 6.3: In-depth review of a secondary school's Humanities

(Based on personal communication with the headteacher)

Background to the faculty

The Humanities faculty was undergoing a major restructuring. It was the lead faculty in the move to become a specialist school at the time of the review. The bid was submitted in March 2011 with History, Religious Education and Citizenship as lead subjects. This review was carried out while the school awaited the decision to be made by the government. The school was subsequently successful in gaining specialist Humanities status.

Leadership

The aims, values and policies of the Humanities faculty influence the work of staff and form the basis of a shared sense of purpose. The Humanities faculty has clear policies and learning objectives, and focuses on learners' needs, which gives a positive direction to the faculty's work. Leadership of the faculty is concentrated on the most important issues – teaching and learning, and ongoing development of a professional culture and learning organisation. There is evidence of shared decision making (shown in the faculty minutes) and collaborative planning to secure faculty involvement. This shows synthesis as a result of monitoring that was evidenced through subsequent planning and decision making. Leadership is strong from the head of faculty, however leadership needs to be developed and encouraged at individual subject level: Citizenship, RE and Geography. The faculty is beginning to generate its own momentum for continued improvement.

Management and organisation

Each department within the faculty had been involved in effective development planning linked to audits of strengths and weaknesses. Priorities in the development plan have been defined in terms of more precise target setting allocated to specific people, realistically costed in terms of time, personnel and resources and related to training and support needs. The faculty has open and clear lines of communication networks that allow for the free flow of ideas and information between staff.

Staff development

The Humanities faculty needs to develop a well-defined and coordinated policy on staff development. This will involve the faculty systematically and frequently undertaking a careful analysis of its training needs. Arrangements for performance management are fully in place and have a direct effect on staff development.

Monitoring process within the faculty

Mechanisms for monitoring the quality of teaching and learning, assessment procedures and data collection of such assessments, tests and exams is supported by a whole-school approach. This needs to be developed and the frequency and methods of reporting on progress be determined. The faculty will need to address underachievement, raise expectations and improve against its previous best. There are regular reviews of learner progress during faculty meetings, where all staff are involved in decisions regarding learner movement. Once established, all review processes need to have a clear focus on improvement in the classroom. The faculty has demonstrated that it is beginning to develop effective monitoring and evaluation processes and that these are becoming embedded. The faculty shows an understanding of the review process as evidenced against improvement in results.

Parental/community involvement

The faculty does not have a systematic approach to monitoring parental and learner views, although these are gathered at whole-school level and feedback is given to departments. This is an area the faculty needs to develop. The faculty may find it useful to produce an annual newsletter for parents, setting out the commitment expected of learners, parents/carers and of the faculty itself. In this way clear guidance can be given to parents on policies, plans, curriculum events and procedures. The faculty keeps parents fully informed about their child's progress, potential and achievement in line with school policy, but there is a need for effective communication through various school documentation including the school prospectus and the school website. The faculty needs to develop links with local companies (e.g. HSBC Bank, ASDA) to be involved with teachers undertaking mock interviews for Year 11 students for example, and to encourage the use of community volunteers to support learning and enrich the curriculum.

◯ Discussion: Case study 6.3

Case study 6.3 demonstrates the need to develop policy and practice that is underpinned by holistic awareness and 'buy-in' to the vision and mission statement from all staff at the school to make it work for them and their learners. There is strong leadership that enables each faculty head to develop their own leadership style to facilitate change in their own area. Here, the need to recognise the potential of staff, their strengths and their development needs for personal growth is high on the agenda so that their focus remains on providing the highest quality learning experiences for their learners. This collegial approach based in team work is a strong message from this case study, showing the need to move away from the silo mentality or lone-leader approach to doing things that is, thankfully, slowly disappearing in our schools. This is replaced in this case study school by an enabling, 'can-do' culture, with very close attention paid to monitoring, evaluation and improvement of policies and practice (Bell and Stevenson, 2006).

As noted by Bell and Stevenson (2006: 143), the leaders (head, senior team and faculty heads) paid huge service to action rather than rhetoric or lip service, which enabled all to take a deeply held conviction of team work, achieving success for all and working with the wider community. A point to remember is that policy development and QA are intertwined, as they form complex elements of school development strategy and the process of change management. At any one time, the leaders, governors and staff have to simultaneously make sense of their internal workings against external policy agendas, respond to factors close to their own context and develop and pursue their own agenda. Such developments may lead to tensions between the external factors and internal factors that require accountability. According to Bell and Stevenson (2006: 142), leadership has to operationalise values, linking leadership, strategy and policy. This, we believe, requires good internal QA systems to be put into place that are easily understood and applied by staff.

Being aware of teachers' rights, responsibilities and legal liabilities – and how this enables QA

This section briefly explores some of the issues about teachers' rights in general terms, rather than from a legal perspective of contracts. This is because it is important for us to know how our responsibilities link to the duty of care we have to our learners and the need for QA to monitor progress. The Teachers' Standards for use in schools in England were implemented in September 2012. These standards define the minimum level of practice expected of trainees and teachers from the point of being awarded qualified teacher status (QTS) (DfE, 2011).

The Department for Education (DfE) and the Welsh Government are responsible for education and children's services in England and Wales. According to the DfE (2016), everyone in the teaching sector has an employment contract with their school/college. A contract is an agreement that sets out an employee's employment conditions, rights, responsibilities and duties. There is a common understanding that both parties, the employee and employer, adhere to a contract until it ends. This contract is different to 'contract to provide services' like painting someone's shop, which is not an employment contract. Teachers are responsible for their teaching duties and the quality of lesson preparation, delivery and assessment, as part of the QA process. They also have duties as a staff member involving team, departmental or, in primary settings, Key Stage meetings, staff meetings and involvement in curricular activities. Senior staff may also have financial responsibilities.

Teachers' duty of care to pupils means they have legal responsibilities, requiring reasonable care to protect the health, safety and welfare of learners.

Their legal responsibilities derive from three sources: the common-law duty of care (traditionally, the term 'in loco parentis' was used to describe the duty of care that a teacher has towards the learner); the statutory duty of care (this means that teachers are also responsible under the Children Act, which places statutory duties upon those who care for learners to provide safeguarding and to promote the welfare of the learner); and the duty arising from the contract of employment (the planning, preparation and other related teaching duties) (NUT, 2012). For example, there is a strong role for the education service in protecting learners from abuse, and learner protection responsibilities also extend to vulnerable adults. Education bodies have a statutory duty to carry out their functions with a view to safeguarding and promoting the welfare of learners under the Education Act 2002 and accompanying regulations.

Schools (including academies) or colleges should have equal opportunities policies and practices which ensure equal treatment of all employees and which contain provision for complaints to be pursued. Policies should prohibit unlawful discrimination, harassment and bullying of teachers by other teachers or pupils (NUT, 2012: 15). There is a legal requirement to promote equal opportunities and to provide reasonable adjustments for those with disabilities, as provided for in the Equality Act 2010. The term also covers the professional duties of teachers as set out in the statutory School Teachers' Pay and Conditions Document (DfE, 2011).

Equality of opportunities is an ideal for learners and teachers, and it is the responsibility of leaders to ensure that the ideal is put into practice (Coleman, 2002: 135). They can do this through making sure it is on the agenda, talked about and discussed; provide career opportunities for all staff; ensure that interview panels are representative; look at all policies from an equal opportunities perspective, examining language, metaphors, images; link with communities and listen and learn from each other (Burton, 1993).

Implications for educators

Individual schools and teachers need to understand what they may be liable and responsible for in their duty of care to learners to avoid or at least reduce the potential for successful litigation by claimants (Newnham, 2000). For example, if there is an accident, then follow school policy, document as many details as possible including how the accident occurred, the nature of the injuries, who administered first aid, whether an ambulance was called, who was present at the time of the accident, the events leading up to and including the incident, what happened subsequently and who was notified. The document must be signed and dated and a copy kept. It is worth noting that no one wants to accept liability and if they can find someone else to blame they will. Negligence is only one aspect of how the law impacts on the practice of teachers and their responsibilities to learners. Teachers have legal responsibility for the safety of their learners. They are expected to act with caution, sensible leadership and wise guidance (ibid.: 50).

What we have tried to illustrate in this section is the need to be aware of our roles and responsibilities to our learners alongside acting and behaving professionally. This is based on individual integrity by making good judgements; showing respect to others; taking reasonable care to ensure the safety and welfare of learners and colleagues; continuing learning (Wood and Dickinson, 2010: 93).

Bringing it all together: Policies, procedures, ethos and action

Hopefully you have drawn some ideas together about what quality assurance means and how the area is fraught with slippery language and contradiction. There are many QA approaches available, and there is no 'one-size-fits-all' action plan or template to hang your ideas on. Rather, we have suggested a few ideas for you to consider in your discussion with colleagues. It is paramount that all settings have an educational policy which is monitored and evaluated for quality assurance and audit. To move from policy and procedures of quality assurance to action, we develop Lumby and Coleman's (2016: 169–186) ideas of: ethos and culture; building capacity in staff, learners and parents; goals and actions.

Each school has its own ethos and culture unique to itself and its locale. This is important, as illustrated by this example of a multi-cultural school. Aldridge School (fictitious name) is in the Midlands with 95 per cent black and ethnic minority students. It is located in a very mixed Muslim and small African-Caribbean population, resulting in skewed ethnic profiles in nearby schools. The school's values strongly resonate with social justice ideals of fairness and human rights. It has a strong inclusive culture where everyone in the community is valued and a strong focus on teaching and learning. This is shown by the high level of learner engagement in the life of the school. It has a strong anti-racist policy supported by a high degree of confidence in the operation of this policy by staff, students and parents.

The ethos of building capacity in staff, learners and parents gives a good framework to set goals and actions to be monitored. Building capacity means changing people's mindsets in order to build a positive capacity for helpful attitudes and behaviour towards the ethos. This may take time and requires challenging everyone.

Summary

This chapter illustrates the importance of school policy agendas and the need to put in place quality assurance procedures for effective monitoring and evaluation as part of accountability. These are shaped by the values and commitment of school leaders. Strong leadership at all levels of the school system makes things happen and it is inevitable that change produces tensions and sometimes resistance which needs to be managed through effective communication procedures and building good relationships. We saw that school leaders take every opportunity to scan the environment to ensure there is some alignment between internal and external policies. Good leaders will manage this well based on their own needs analysis, their own context and their own culture, shaped by their values and commitment to high-quality learner experiences and outcomes. We saw the need for key actions to shape policies on the rights and responsibilities of teachers and learners to reflect and accommodate particular contextual factors. We have adapted Lumby and Coleman's (2016: 184) ideas to suggest that leaders should:

- agree on QA procedures that are understood in the school;
- build a culture of a 'can-do' attitude by building the capacity of staff through distributive activities;
- work to make high expectations a reality through policies, structures and action;
- give responsibility for scrutinising monitoring data to a number of people, thus gaining viewpoints from different perspectives.

References

Bell, L. and Stevenson, H. (2006) Citizenship and social justice: Developing education policy in multi-ethnic schools. In *Education Policy: Process, Themes and Impact*. Abingdon: Routledge.

Burton, L. (1993) 'Management, 'race' and gender: An unlikely alliance?' *British Educational Research Journal,* 19 (3): 275–290.

Businessballs: www.businessballs.com

Coleman, M. (2002) Managing for equal opportunities. In T. Bush and L. Bell (eds) *The Principles of Educational Leadership and Management,* 2nd edn. London: Sage.

Cotterill, T. (2016) Accountability. In A. O'Grady and V. Cottle (eds) *Exploring Education at Postgraduate Level – Policy, Theory and Practice.* London: David Fulton, pp. 142–150.

Department for Business, Energy and Industrial Strategy (BIS): www.bis.gov.uk

Department for Education (DfE): www.education.gov.uk

Department for Education (DfE) (2010) *The Importance of Teaching: The Schools White Paper.* London: DfE.

Department for Education (DfE) (2011) *Teachers' Standards Guidance for School Leaders, School Staff and Governing Bodies.* London: DfE.

Department for Education (DfE) (2016) Employment contract. Available at https://www.gov.uk/employment-contracts-and-conditions/overview (accessed 30 October 2016).

Fullan, M. (2004) *Leading in a Culture of Change: Personal Action Guide and Workbook.* San Francisco: Jossey Bass.

House of Commons Children, Schools and Families Committee (2009) *School Accountability.* London: The Stationery Office.

Lumby, J. and Coleman, M. (2016) *Leading for Equality: Making Schools Fairer.* London: Sage.

Muijs, D. and Harris, A. (2006) Teacher-led school improvement: Teacher leadership in the UK. *Teaching and Teacher Education,* 22 (8): 961–972.

National Union of Teachers (NUT) (2012) *NUT Notes: Education, the Law and You.* Available at https://www.teachers.org.uk/files/the-law-and-you--8251-.pdf (accessed 30 October 2016).

Newnham, H. (2000) When is a teacher or school liable in negligence? *Australian Journal of Teacher Education*, 25 (1): 1–51.

O'Sullivan, H. and West-Burnham, J. (eds) (2011) *Leading and Managing Schools.* London: Sage.

Szabo, M. and Lambert, L. (2002) The preparation of new constructivist leaders. In L. Lambert, D. Walker; D. P. Zimmerman, J. E. Cooper, M. Dale Lambert, M. E. Gardner and M. Szabo (eds) *The Constructivist Leader.* New York: Teachers College Press, pp. 204–238.

West, A., Mattei, P. and Roberts, J. (2011) Accountability and sanctions in English schools. *British Journal of Educational Studies*, 59 (1): 41–62.

West-Burnham, J. (1994) Quality. In T. Bush and J. West-Burnham, J. (eds) *The Principles of Educational Management*. Harlow: Longman.

Wood, J. and Dickinson, J. (2011) *Quality Assurance and Evaluation in the Lifelong Learning Sector.* Exeter: Learning Matters.

7 Responding to users

Learners', parents' and carers' voices

Chapter aims

When you have finished reading this chapter you will be able to:

1. explain the significance of learner and parent/carer voice to internal staff and other outside agencies;
2. identify different ways organisations can capture learner and parent/carer voice and use this information to inform and develop policy and practice;
3. describe the skills needed by staff to enable them to become skilled listeners so that they can work effectively with diverse groups of education users;
4. explain the importance and impact of learner and parent/carer voice to the learning environment.

Overview of chapter

This chapter examines the way in which education organisations, as a result of changing attitudes, greater public awareness and Ofsted guidelines, have been obliged to pay more attention to the ideas and thoughts of education users: that is learners, parents and carers themselves. It is no longer acceptable for schools, colleges or any other education setting to act in an autocratic or god-like way, claiming to know 'what is best' for learners and their families and ignoring the wishes and feelings of the communities they serve. Education settings need to recognise that their reason for being is to 'provide a public service' (Bright Ideas Management, 1988: 9) and consequently learner, home and community consultation is absolutely essential. Education settings must find ways to reach out to users to systematically collect their thoughts in order to inform policy, develop organisational procedures and update practices. Organisations need to establish formal and other opportunities to obtain learner and home views. Information collection must be wide-reaching, not restricted to the opinions of a cooperative, articulate or vociferous few. Organisations must also find ways to collect the views of potentially vulnerable groups such as disabled users, students with SEN or minority populations.

Key words: consultation; home; learner/student voice; listening; parents/carers.

Introduction

The still current 1988 Education Reform Act introduced local management of schools (LMS), which reduced the powers of LEAs to instruct education organisations to carry out home and community consultations and provided schools, colleges and other education settings with the freedom to choose who they talked to. However, while LMS ostensibly grants increased autonomy for education settings, simultaneously Ofsted's 2015 common inspection framework requires organisations to engage with 'parents, carers and employers [to] help them understand how children and learners are doing in relation to the standards expected and what they need to do to improve' (2015: 13). Other research on student well-being (Kher et al., 1999; Korobkin, 1988; Woods, 1976) has demonstrated that learners make better progress when they have the opportunity to voice their thoughts to staff.

Although the inspection framework no longer formally requires settings to report in advance on learner views in their self-evaluation forms (SEFs) or to formally meet with student councils, student and community voice still forms an important part of the inspection process, as inspectors contact parents and carers prior to an inspection to seek their views and inspectors will routinely talk with learners during observations to determine their opinions. Thus, because of the external assessment regime, organisations are locked into a system where they need to be aware of the views of education users and they need to show how they are responding to any issues raised. Even though organisations have a statutory duty to collect information on learner and family views, good providers both recognise their ethical obligations to understand the communities they serve and appreciate that the more they value their communities, the better they will be able to meet their needs. Information collection is not seen as a burden but as a vital tool in improving provision and enhancing the learning experience of all.

Learner/student voice

Learner voice has become increasingly important for all education settings. The significance of voice is enshrined in Article 12 of the United Nations Convention on the Rights of the Child (UNCRC) which states:

> Parties shall assure to the child who is capable of forming his or her views the right to express those views freely in all matters affecting the child, the views of the child being given due weight in accordance with the age and maturity of the child ... The child

shall in particular be provided the opportunity to be heard in any judicial and administrative proceedings affecting the child.

(United Nations, 1989: Article 12)

The UK unconditionally signed the Convention in 1990 and 'is therefore legally obliged to give effect to it in full' (Lundy, 2007: 928). The implications of adopting the Convention are far-reaching for it requires that *children themselves* (not their parents, guardians, carers or proxy adults such as headteachers and teachers) are consulted and involved in decisions about their care and welfare. Even though the Convention contains the caveat that 'age and maturity' should be taken into account, it establishes a presumption that children and young people should routinely be involved in all matters, including education, which concern them. The Convention echoes the slogan of disability campaigners of 'nothing about us, without us' and is based on the premise 'it is the *right* of children and young people to have a say about things that concern them' (Thomson, 2008: 1). Education has an obligation and a real opportunity to move beyond 'minimalist, tokenistic opportunities to participate and engage' (Lundy, 2007: 929) and involve all learners in meaningful conversation about their educational futures. Learners should not be reduced to hapless bystanders who have little to no understanding of their daily realities.

Establishing dialogue with learners

Although there is much good practice in the Early Years sector where each child is seen as an individual and is at the centre of all learning experiences, in other sectors (primary, secondary and further education), 'the average student's experience of [learning] involved being placed in a passive learning environment' (Rajeeb, 2009: 23) where contributions are neither encouraged nor welcomed. Rather than being driven by learning outcomes and targets, Early Years practitioners seek to adopt a holistic approach to development and, through dialogue with the child, construct learning experiences led by the child's needs and wishes. However, this practice is not universally adopted in all sectors.

Fuelled partly by Article 12, partly by government and Ofsted's interest in learner voice; and partly by changing societal attitudes, practices are now changing in other sectors and settings. Consequently, many are now taking a much greater interest in learner voice and 'have introduced … participation strategies into their educational systems' (Flutter, 2007: 345).

Learner voice matters and, as the direct recipients of education, learners comprehend education systems intimately. Further, 'while[learners] may not be the voice of academia or authority, they are the authentic voice of experience and perhaps understand more than anyone else how it feels to be a … [learner] in the … education system' (Peart, 2013: 123).

As such learners hold vital information which, if effectively tapped, can be used to help design (or redesign) the learning environment and teaching approaches.

Moreover, what learners 'have to say about their own experiences of learning are not only worth listening to but [provide] … a foundation … [for] improving' settings (Hopkins, 2010: 40). However, speaking out in education can imply risk for learners and because of 'issues of power and voice' (Cremin et al., 2011: 586), where educators are routinely accorded more power than learners, some learners may be fearful of stating their opinions. Indeed, some educators appear to actively 'disregard [learners'] views' (ibid.: 587) configuring it as 'undermining their professional autonomy' (ibid.). Building on the good practice in Early Years, education leaders in other sectors need to create an environment which welcomes and embraces learner contributions so, together, learners and educators can co-construct learning opportunities. Lundy identified four key elements that need to be in place to encourage learner dialogue:

- Space: … the opportunity to express a view;
- Voice: … facilitated to express their views;
- Audience: the view must be listened to; and
- Influence: the view must be acted on.

(Lundy, 2007: 933)

Safe spaces where learners are given permission to openly use their voice are vital in collecting information and educators must establish temporal and physical spaces for learners to express their opinions. These spaces may already exist within organisations (for example dedicated tutor time where learners are given the opportunity to provide feedback on a variety of issues) or they may need to be established (such as setting up a school council). Such spaces need to fulfil their primary objective of collecting information and sufficient time needs to be allocated to enable this to happen. This might involve changing timetables to make opportunities for dialogue available, setting up drop-in surgeries for learners where they can air their views, or considering models of delegated responsibility (where named learners collect the views of others) to make effective use of time. Such a time-saving model is often adopted in the running of learner/student councils. Physical space also requires attention and should ideally be a clean, spacious area with comfortable furnishings. Establishing appropriate areas could also involve setting up 'staff-free' zones managed and controlled by the learners.

In many ways, each of the four features identified by Lundy is inter-related with and influenced by the other. Learners need to be given appropriate support to help them first voice their opinions and then hone their views so they can be widely shared; a temporal and physical space must be available to use their voice; an audience with institutional influence that is prepared to acknowledge concerns needs to be present; and any issues raised must actually be appropriately handled and be seen to be managed. Each of the four features is like part of an interlocking jigsaw – each piece can exist independently, but full understanding of learner voice and subsequent change which responds to this voice can only be achieved when all four features are present. As such there is no single 'correct' starting point and organisations must begin action at a point which is contextually practical and meets the needs of the setting. This could involve defining communication channels so information is passed to appropriate staff or organising election of learner representatives. Consequently, to an extent, disaggregating the four features represents an artificial division and the significance of each key element (voice, space, audience and influence) is embedded in the following discussions.

If educators are to engage in meaningful dialogue with learners, discussions which have the possibility of promoting change and enhancing both teaching and learning environments, leaders must ensure these four features are securely in place. Only then can learners begin to take part in articulating their views and influence the shape of their learning environment.

Learning to listen and valuing learner voice. Most educators recognise the significance of listening and 80 per cent of teachers believe that listening skills are important (Campbell, 2011: 66). Educators are used to talking and are used to being listened to. Indeed, many educators, by virtue of their position, expect to be listened to by learners, parents, carers and other professionals. However, not all educators afford this same privilege to others and some appear to lack listening skills. While most educators intuitively understand 'listening as a vital communication function, it is still frequently ignored' (Weinrauch and Swanda, 1975: 26) and some educators appear content to act without taking the time to collect information from others. This is a real concern for education leaders. Unless educators take the time to understand the needs and wishes of those they work with, they will not be able to secure the best outcomes for learners, their families and the learning communities they work with. Learning to listen is vital in supporting learners to use their voice and access an audience.

In their research for Ulster University, Dixon and O'Hara identified seven key active listening skills, shown in abridged form below, needed by all education workers:

- Stop talking – listen openly to the other person.
- Remove distractions.
- Be receptive.
- Delay evaluation of what you have heard until you fully understand it.
- Try not to be defensive.
- Maintain attention. Be patient.
- Ask the other person for as much detail as he/she can provide.

(University of Ulster, n.d.: 11)

Educators need to practise and develop these skills so they can accurately hear what learners and their families have to say to help improve 'the process of teaching and learning' (Hopkins, 2008: 400) for all.

⯑ **Reflective questions**

1. How good are you at listening to learners and their families? How do you know this?
2. What skills do you employ to help learners or their families share information with you?
3. What additional skills do you need to develop to help you become a better listener?
4. As an education leader, how have you helped your staff teams develop their listening skills?

Q **Discussion: Seriously listening and being a receptive audience**

Taking the time to reflect on your personal skill set is an important professional development activity. You need to know and understand your existing personal strengths and areas for future development. Active listening is an essential skill for all educators in every sector from Early Years through to further education. Listening to learners is a vital part of data collection and more fully understanding learning communities. Failure to listen risks acting on incomplete data and will not enable you to provide the best possible learning experiences. Further, it compromises the integrity of learner voice and removes learners' access to audience.

Learners and their families are central in all education settings from nurseries through to colleges. Learners know, through lived experience, the realities of attending a particular setting. They understand the strengths of an organisation and know where improvements are needed. By working with learners, educators can enrich their understanding and can use this data to construct a fuller, deeper conception of the setting. Such data can be used reactively to solve difficulties when problems arise, or proactively to prevent issues from occurring.

When listening to learners it is important educators choose the most appropriate venue, a place where learners feel comfortable so they can easily talk. It is unlikely education staff will gain in-depth information from a few seconds of snatched conversation in the corridor and they should use neutral territory or consider leaving the 'educator zone' and venture into the learner zone. Every day learners talk to educators in teacher territory, a venue where they may not feel very relaxed. Changing the venue can change the nature of interactions and may produce more productive outcomes. Remember, as adults, some educators may be physically taller than their learners and need to sit down so both educator and learners are at a similar height. Education staff should also remove physical barriers such as tables which can impede conversation, and give learners time to think. Learners may offer some surprising replies if allowed sufficient time to frame their responses. If learners are struggling for words, educators could offer suggestions which might describe the learners' experiences, but should avoid taking over and dominating the conversation.

Learners want to be involved in their education. However, they can only be involved if they are given opportunities to do so. Leaders need to work with staff teams to engineer opportunities for dialogue. This may mean altering practices, or working in a different way but without change there can be no progression. It is through actively listening to learners that their voice achieves full effect and can promote new ways of working.

Learner and student councils – spaces to talk

In order to 'consult with young people' (Wyness, 2009: 536) and facilitate discussion between setting staff and learners, many settings have introduced learner or student councils, and 'at least 90% of schools now use them' (Bennett, 2012). Councils are formal bodies that act as an interface between education staff and learners and are a 'tangible manifestation of pupil voice' (Whitty and Wisby, 2007). There is no set model for learner councils and each organisation can establish its own parameters including how many and which learners can sit on the council; how often the council meets; the nature of staff representation on the council; and what topics are discussed by the council. How the council is perceived and received by both learners and staff will be influenced by the level of engagement provided by the council. The challenge for education leaders is how the council will be constituted, how to avoid 'connecting mainly with the interests and voices of a minority of [the] privileged and advantaged' (Wyness, 2009: 549) and how to use information collected to benefit all learners. Learner and student councils support all four elements identified by Lundy (2007): they provide the space for learners to use their voice, an audience for that voice to be heard and can have an influential effect in role in decision making.

When working with children and young people, Hart identified seven levels of participation, shown in Table 7.1, ranging from decoration (where young people have no effective voice at all) through to collaborative decision making with adults.

A key role for education leaders is what training will be given to learners so they can take an active role in learner councils – 'this is essential if pupils are to contribute effectively to decision making' (Whitty and Wisby, 2007). Learners need to be supported in how to frame contributions so they are heard. Equally councils should be constructed so older learners are not allowed to dominate proceedings. While including learner voice may represent a new way of working, some settings have fully embraced this concept and now even routinely include learners in staff appointment panels, recognising that learners 'bring a unique and important perspective to the process of decision making' (Kent, 2012: 149).

Table 7.1 Children's participation from tokenism to citizenship (adapted from Hart, 1992: 8–14)

Degrees of participation	**Child-initiated, shared decisions with adults**	Children have the ideas, set up the project, and invite adults to join with them in making decisions.
	Child-initiated and directed	Children have the initial idea and decide how the project is to be carried out. Adults are available but do not take charge.
	Adult-initiated, shared decisions with children	Adults have the initial idea but children are involved in every step of the planning and implementation. Not only are their views considered, but they are also involved in taking the decisions.
	Consulted and informed	The project is designed and run by adults but children are consulted. They have a full understanding of the process and their opinions are taken seriously.
	Assigned but informed	Adults decide on the project and children volunteer for it. The children understand the project, and know who decided they should be involved and why. Adults respect their views.
Non-participation	**Tokenism**	Children are asked to say what they think about an issue but have little or no choice about the way they express those views or the scope of the ideas they can express.
	Decoration	Children take part in an event, for example by singing, dancing or wearing T-shirts with logos on, but they do not really understand the issues.
	Manipulation	Children do or say what adults suggest they do, but have no real understanding of the issues, or children are asked what they think, adults use some of their ideas but do not tell them what influence they have had on the final decision.

Case study 7.1: Council work

Ethan has learning difficulties and an EHC plan. He is in Year 4 of his local primary school. When a vacancy on the school council became available, supported by his school friends and a teaching assistant (TA), Ethan ran a successful campaign and was duly elected. At Ethan's school the council was organised by key stage with two pupil representatives, one boy and one girl, from each year group. Ethan was in the upper school council with other pupils from Years 3 to 6. The upper school council met once every half term, with full council meetings of upper and lower school taking place once a term. The final full council meeting of the year also served as an annual review and future planning meeting. Council meetings were facilitated and chaired by one of the school learning mentors as the school had made a conscious decision that teachers may appear to be authority figures and could stifle discussions.

Although nervous about attending council meetings, assisted by a TA who helped him to prepare, Ethan was looking forward to taking part. He worked with the TA and the female representative for Year 4 to collect the views of other pupils about the new outdoor play equipment and menu choices for school dinners. After the first council meeting, Ethan reported to his TA that the meetings were 'just taken over by the big kids'. The TA talked this situation through with Ethan and advised him to persist as the situation would probably settle down. However, having attended four council meetings Ethan has told the TA 'there is no point in going, nobody listens unless you are a Year 6' and the council does not 'talk about anything that really matters to pupils'. Ethan has said he does not want to be on the council any more as 'it makes no difference'.

Reflective questions

1. How does your setting organise its school council? If your setting does not have a council, why/how was this decision reached?
2. What support is provided for students with SEN in your setting so they may actively participate on the council?
3. What action could be taken to improve the operation of the council so it runs more effectively?

Discussion: Mending the council

On one level it seems Ethan's school were concerned with promoting inclusion and established structures which enabled Ethan to be elected to the school council. The TA was pivotal in this situation, recognising that as Ethan had SEN he may require additional support in preparing for meetings. However, from Ethan's reports it appears the council has not been truly inclusive, ignoring both him and other younger pupils. Ethan's school has not secured the safe space for all pupils to voice their concerns or provided a receptive audience for all learner views.

Settings must consider which member of staff is the most appropriate facilitator – placing a junior member of staff in this role may give the impression the council is not important, but placing a senior member of staff in charge could scare some learners away. This is a difficult balance to achieve and settings could, in the spirit of open participation, consult learners and ask who they would choose as a meeting facilitator. In this example it seems the learning mentor lacked experience of running meetings and did not know how to obtain views from all learners. School councils are important bodies and need to be treated seriously by school management. They need to be run by experienced facilitators who possess the skills needed to ensure all pupils have an opportunity to participate. Ethan had taken the time to collect the views of his peers; it is important for him to be given the chance to share these views. It is only with the support of a skilled facilitator that all students can be heard and can start to influence decisions made in the school.

To further support participation, the school could consider having a rotating pupil chair or deputy so all year groups have the opportunity to help lead the meeting. Fixed and standing agendas can also assist engagement, with each year representative being asked to state the views of their year group. Further, learners can help to construct council agendas by submitting items for discussion in advance of the meeting. These simple strategies would help to avoid domination by any particular year group or individual.

If the council is to achieve its function of being a vehicle to enable learners to actively engage with decision making and to have an impact on organisational life, it is vital that all learners are supported to actively contribute to discussions. Organisations will need to work out the best ways to achieve this and the first and most logical action would be to ask the learners themselves what would be needed to make the council a more effective group capable of having an impact on the organisation.

Communication between home and settings

It is important for all settings to recognise that 'parents and families [exert] major influences' (Cunningham and Davis, 1985: 2) on a learner's development and progress. Families are often a child's first teacher and the home environment continues to play a significant role throughout learners' lives. For a learner's development it is important they receive a coherent message from both home and school and there is consistency in approach between the two. However, settings may sometimes act in a way which undermines home values and, similarly, homes may contradict teaching delivered in settings. This can create confusion for learners who may not know who to trust or what to believe. Learners benefit most when there is good communication between home and the setting and when the learner, home and the setting understand one another's roles, responsibilities and capacities. Clear communication avoids confusion and prevents setting up unrealistic expectations or unachievable aspirations. It is important for organisations to work out 'how professionals can work in partnership' (Gascoigne, 1995: 26) with the home, building on each other's strengths to purposefully and holistically support the development of each learner. As the 'legal guardians of their children and as such ultimately responsible for them in all ways' (Cunningham and Davis, 1985: 2), parents and carers have a right to know what is happening in settings and what it means for them and their children.

Education organisations are used to contacting families and giving them information about a myriad of different issues from trips, to fundraising to new school buildings. However, sometimes this communication may seem one-sided or simply be provided as information. Frequently no response is invited from home and often none is expected. This uneven distribution of authority can disempower families and homes who may begin to feel the settings do not take 'their opinions seriously' (Ofsted, 2011: 13). Ofsted expect settings to involve home but, crucially, such involvement is only considered successful if it makes a positive difference to students' learning. Leaders need to ensure information is shared openly and regularly so families can play a real role in the education of their children.

Capturing parent/carer voice

Most families want to be involved in their children's education and recognised as significant partners with valuable contributions to make. However, some settings seem 'intimidating to many people' (Bright Ideas Management, 1988: 11), populated by distant, busy professionals who do not appear to have the time or inclination to talk with parents and carers. Some people, possibly damaged by their own educational experiences, may even be too afraid to even venture into a school, college or nursery, seeing them as the sole preserve of professionals. In order to dismantle these real or perceived barriers, leaders need to find different ways of making families feel welcome and to actively encourage their contributions. It is important that settings adopt a range of approaches to capture parental/carer voice as one method alone may not work for all family groups. It is also important for leaders to remember that some families work varying shift patterns and as far as possible organisations should offer the same event at different times so they can reach as many families as possible.

Table 7.2 shows some common contact mechanisms used by education settings. It indicates the range of contact systems available to organisations, from the traditional letter home to more innovative approaches such as conference calls. Not all these approaches will work for all homes so settings will need to experiment to discover the most productive forms of communication. While all communication systems may be useful to the organisation, some mechanisms are better than others for collecting home/family feedback. For harder to reach families, none of the systems listed may work and organisations may have to develop bespoke, dedicated approaches to contact some families.

Table 7.2 Home-setting contact mechanisms

Type of contact	Appropriate uses	Ways to capture parent/carer voice
1. Introduction or welcome events	These are greeting events to welcome new or prospective families to the setting. They can be used to introduce families to the staff, provide information about how the organisation is run and managed and offer buildings tours.	Depending on how the event is organised, staff could circulate and meet families to gather their views or feedback sheets could be distributed at or after the event. It is important for leaders to collate these views once the event has finished.
2. Issue-specific events	These events have a single issue focus, such as an overseas visit or a new education-based immunisation programme. Parents and carers are invited in to hear presentations or view exhibitions at the setting to explain the focus issue.	Often these events gather all visitors together in a single hall/room and invite open questions from the audience. Although a brave minority may ask questions, leaders should consider how to collect the views of those who remain silent. Modern voting-type technology may be useful here or questions could be posted online after the event with settings committing to providing an answer in a specified time frame.
3. Celebration events	These events are an opportunity for the whole learning community to come together to celebrate a specific issue. This may be a routine event such as the end of year or could mark an occasional episode such as a new building opening.	Education staff can mingle with families and use the event to informally capture feedback from the assembled audience. It is important leaders collect these comments after the event to close the feedback loop.
4. Learner reporting sessions (aka parents' or consultation evenings)	Most families want to know how their children are doing in school, both academically and socially. Learner reporting sessions provide an opportunity to share this information in person.	At these events staff must be encouraged to speak *with* (rather than *at*) families and actively seek to explore which topics families are interested in.
5. Home/setting reporting books	Reporting books are a good way of establishing a regular two-way dialogue between home and the setting. Any relevant topics can be noted in the reporting book and questions asked (and answered) by both sides. Reporting books are in common use in Early Years, primary and secondary settings and for students with SEN.	Parents or carers need to be encouraged to take shared ownership of such reporting books and to treat them as a communication tool between home and the setting, raising any points they feel are relevant.
6. Letters	This is a common and very useful mechanism for sharing information between the setting and home about a variety of matters.	Although it is possible to gain feedback by including a reply slip on a letter, this tends to be a very one-sided approach to communication between a setting and home.
7. Comment boxes	Comment boxes, which need to be placed in a prominent position, are a useful tool for capturing emergent or contemporary burning issues.	Comment cards (with envelopes if anonymity is important) and pens should be placed next to the boxes to encourage contributions. Large signs should also be displayed inviting comments from families and home.
8. Open-door policies	Open-door policies can be a first stage in removing potential barriers between the setting and the home. They are a useful way of collecting incidental as well as significant information in an informal way.	Open doors remove the formality of pre-booked meetings and staff and families can meet on an ad-hoc basis to discuss any points they wish to.
9. Parental surveys	Surveys are used to gather information from all families on the running of the setting or other significant points. Many settings organise annual or biannual surveys to collect data from home.	Written feedback captured in this way provides a useful database of family attitudes and potential concerns.
10. Digital contact	Increasingly, education settings are 'using email, mobile telephones and the internet to reach parents more easily, including parents … not living with their children' (Ofsted, 2011: 4). Families can take part in Skype or conference calls removing the need to attend reporting events in person.	If settings choose to use Skype or conference calls to gather feedback, these tend to only work effectively with limited numbers or small groups of people.

One of the longest established ways of engaging parents and carers in the life of education organisations is via Parent Teacher Associations (PTAs). Although PTAs are common in the primary and secondary sector they are less prevalent in Early Years or further education. While such an association should present an ideal opportunity to gather the voice of an assembled collection of parents and carers, 'the proportion of parents actively involved [is] usually small' (Ofsted, 2011: 22). Further, some families cannot, for a number of reasons, engage with this group. PTAs are not, therefore, representative of all families. Moreover, PTAs are sometimes only narrowly configured as a fundraising group and are not given the opportunity to 'contribute much to the [settings'] development of policy' (ibid.).

? Reflective questions

1. What forms of communication does your setting use to contact homes?
2. In what way is this influenced by the learners' ages and/or abilities?
3. What are the most and least successful forms of communication? Has any action been taken to explore why some forms are more or less successful than others?

Q Discussion: Keeping in touch

Education leaders need a range of strategies to ensure they can contact home. Often leaders will inherit an existing range of mechanisms. Sometimes, it may seem more convenient to retain current systems. If these have worked well, with homes being fully informed of all relevant matters and feedback arriving from families, it may not be necessary for leaders to take any action.

However, leaders should at least monitor communication systems to ensure they continue to work well. Leaders need to, periodically, review all communication mechanisms and interrogate how well each system is working and how that system is being used. This should form part of the settings quality review systems. For example, if letters are sent home, who is the messenger? Are letters given to learners to take home? Are learners sufficiently mature to be given this responsibility? If settings rely on satchel post, can they be confident letters arrive safely? Although learners are often asked to take letters home, some learners are not capable of completing this task and it may be more appropriate that information is recorded in a learner reporting book which may be less likely to be lost.

If settings are not bothered about lost letters, then the setting needs to question why send a letter at all? Homes are busy places. Sending out information which has no significance is a pointless exercise; it is wasteful of resources and shows little respect to busy families who need to take time to read worthless information. If settings continue to send out hollow letters, homes may disengage with written communication entirely and could miss important information. Settings need to maintain an economic discipline sending as much information as is useful while not withholding key data or overloading homes with irrelevant trivia. Settings also need to be clear on how they assess essential and non-essential information. If settings wish to adopt a 'for information only' approach, then they should review how such information is shared. It may be better to adopt e-messages for general communication, reserving letters for personal information and using secure delivery systems for critical details.

Appraising communication mechanisms allows settings to make informed decisions on how to work with homes and the most effective way of sending and receiving information. If comment boxes only contain an old bus ticket inside, evidence would suggest they are serving no purpose. However, before removal, settings need to explore where the box was sited. Even if the setting decides to remove the box, this should be kept under review and may be reinstated at a later time.

To ensure effective home communication, settings need to put the learner at the centre and use dedicated messaging systems which reflect the capabilities and needs of the learner and contemporary electronic media.

Case study 7.2: Tom's letter

Mr Jones, Tom's father, has contacted the school. He is angry because he had promised Tom that when the time arrived, he would be able to go on a popular (but non-academically essential) field trip to the Peak District, as his elder brother (who attends the same school) had. Because it is non-essential, the trip is organised on a 'first-come-first-served' basis. Mr Jones was aware the trip would be happening sometime in the autumn term but claims he only learned of the dates when another parent informed him the trip was full and no further pupils would be allowed to attend as the youth hostel had no more room. After discussing the situation with his son, Mr Jones learned that Tom had been given a letter about the trip and told to take it home. However, Tom had lost the letter and then forgotten about it. Tom is now upset because his elder brother went on this trip and he feels he has missed out. Mr Jones blames the school for trusting a teenage boy with an important letter and feels the school has a responsibility to let Tom attend. Tom does not have special needs.

? **Reflective questions**

1. How does your setting send out non-essential information?
2. What 'reasonable adjustments' (as the Equality Act requires) does your setting make for students with SEN?
3. What responsibility does the school have towards Tom and his family?

Q Discussion: Tom's trip

This is a difficult situation. The school has to manage Mr Jones' anger and Tom's disappointment. The field trip to the Peak District is an optional extra and does not form part of the academic or assessed curriculum. As such, the school decided a letter was the most appropriate form of communication and felt learners who were interested in the trip should take responsibility for the safe delivery of the letter. Because places for the trip have filled, it is apparent that a number of learners were able to accept this responsibility and safely deliver their letters home.

Mr Jones promised Tom he would be able to go on the trip. However, Mr Jones was aware from previous experience this was a popular excursion. He also knew the visit took place in the autumn term and places were allocated on a 'first-come-first-served' basis. In this regard Mr Jones may have had more information than families without other children. Because Mr Jones is not responsible for organising the trip it is not within his capacity to promise a place to his son, even though he may wish this. As Mr Jones was aware the trip took place in the autumn and he wanted his son to attend, it would have been helpful if he had been more vigilant and checked with Tom on a regular basis if the school had sent out any letters.

To explain this situation to Mr Jones and Tom it would be useful if a middle or senior leader could meet directly with them both at a mutually agreeable time. A middle or senior member of staff meeting directly with the family indicates the school wants to treat this situation seriously and is concerned about both Mr Jones' anger and Tom's unhappiness. As the school cannot compromise health and safety it is unable to automatically give Tom a place on the trip but may be able to put him on a priority waiting list and, should anyone drop out, Tom could attend. Such a meeting is also important as it gives an opportunity to state all parties' responsibilities and expectations.

Tom is a teenager without special needs. He does not require and is not entitled to 'reasonable adjustments'. Consequently, he needs to take responsibility for passing on information. This information needs to be explained to Tom and his family. Although it may be a hard lesson for Tom to miss a school trip, it is important the family understands the extent of the school's responsibilities and that it is not possible to simply give Tom a place. Such a meeting may also provide an incidental opportunity to find out from families how they would prefer non-essential information, like trip details, to be shared. If Tom had SEN, the school should have taken this into account and acted accordingly; this may have involved a personal follow-up telephone call or text or making a note of the trip in Tom's home–school reporting book.

Hard-to-reach families or hard-to-reach organisations?

Some families, possibly as a consequence of previous negative personal history, do not readily engage with education settings. An organisation will find it difficult to meet the needs of all its learners unless it can find ways to involve all families and understand their needs, hopes and aspirations. Organisations should resist the temptation of treating families as a non-differentiated homogenous mass. As all learners are different, so are all family groupings and organisations should use a range of approaches to meet the varying needs of the community. In order to achieve greater involvement, organisations need to have a clear understanding of what is happening for each family and what would help and promote involvement. If the traditional methods of contact detailed in Table 7.2 have not produced positive outcomes, organisations will need to consider other creative means of contact to encourage family engagement. This may mean producing customised communication tools for individual families.

In the first instance it is important to know which families are not engaging. While perceptions may exist on which individuals do not participate in the organisation's life, the accuracy of these views should be checked. Organisations must resist stereotypical assumptions of certain groups or those from certain geographical areas having no interest in education. Organisations need to establish if non-engagement has persisted throughout a young person's educational career or if there was a pivotal moment when participation ceased. In this situation, does the organisation have any knowledge about events which may have prompted disengagement? For example, did a trusted and liked member of staff leave? Is non-engagement absolute or is there contact on some level? For instance, families may willingly attend sporting events where their child is taking part but do not attend parent consultation evenings. Once a clear picture has been determined about which families are not engaging and which forms of communication are least successful, strategies to promote participation can be considered. Organisations need to remember they have an option of leaving the setting and meeting families in different venues. While it may be customary for families to travel to the setting, organisations should not always expect this. Possible alternative contact mechanisms to encourage engagement are detailed in Table 7.3.

Earlier in this chapter Table 7.2 identified traditional means of contacting homes. However, these means may not work for all family groups. Organisations are then obliged

Table 7.3 Alternative strategies to promote engagement for hard-to-reach groups

Strategy	Organisational notes	Benefits of this communication
1. Break-out or road-show events	These are events where the setting leaves its base and sets up a contact point in another venue. This might be a local cafe, community centre or sporting venue. Some leisure centres hold 'family fun nights' and the setting could attend these nights to try to meet with families. If there are periodic events widely attended by the community, education settings should investigate attending these events.	Leaving the organisation's premises enables staff to see families in a different (possibly more positive) way. Families may be happier to attend an event on neutral territory and may be more willing to engage in discussions in these venues.
2. Inter-generational events	These events can be held on school premises or elsewhere. They invite the whole family from the oldest to the very youngest to attend an event which has something for everyone. To a degree, events such as fairs already achieve this task but the offer to the whole family needs to be explicit and there may be a need for changes to provision to cater for the full age range.	These social-type events enable greater bonds to be forged between the organisation and families. They also enable younger family members to be introduced to the setting in an informal way.
3. Training or information sessions	These might include events such as basic car maintenance, an introduction to politics, healthy eating or gardening clubs and can be opened up to the whole family including learners.	In these sessions, children have the opportunity to learn alongside their parents or carers. These events can help to achieve broader aims such as empowering the local community.

to choose whether they will accept this situation or if they will explore other means of contact. Table 7.3 suggests other contact systems organisations could try. Although there is no guarantee these systems will work, they at least provide other avenues to explore.

Summary

This chapter has reviewed issues associated with capturing learner and home voice.

The practice of involving pupils in decision making should not be portrayed as an option which is in the gift of adults but as a legal imperative which is the right of the child.

(Lundy, 2007: 931)

Education leaders must seriously consider how to establish structures and systems which 'enable [learners'] voices to be heard [and] allow them to articulate the interests of their peers' (Wyness, 2009: 540). Leaders must also consider how to enable 'those with significantly less social and cultural capital' (ibid.: 547) such as learners with SEN, younger learners or minority ethnic groups 'to get involved' (ibid.). These are the challenges for education leaders who must recognise they 'do not have a monopoly' (Kent, 2012: 149) on understanding education or identifying future action. Settings need to move away from tokenistic models, and learners and their families need to be encouraged to become 'active, engaged co-constructors of their education' (Rajeeb, 2009: 23).

References

Bennett, T. (2012) School councils: Shut up, we're listening. *Guardian,* 12 March. Available at www.theguardian.com/education/2012/mar/12/school-councils-number-lip-service (accessed 30 August 2016).

Bright Ideas Management (1988) *Parents and Schools.* Leamington Spa: Scholastic.

Campbell, R. (2011) The power of the listening ear. *English Journal,* 100 (5): 66–70.

Cremin, H., Mason, C. and Busher, H. (2011) Problematising pupil voice using visual methods: Findings from a study of engaged and disaffected pupils in an urban secondary school. *British Educational Research Journal,* 37 (4): 585–603.

Cunningham, C. and Davis, H. (1985) *Working with Parents – Frameworks for Collaboration.* Milton Keynes: Open University Press.

Flutter, J. (2007) Teacher development and pupil voice. *The Curriculum Journal,* 18 (3): 343–345.

Gascoigne, E. (1995) *Working with Parents as Partners in SEN.* London: David Fulton.

Hart, R. A. (1992) *Children's Participation from Tokenism to Citizenship.* Florence: UNICEF Innocenti Research Centre.

Hopkins, E. (2008) Classroom conditions to secure enjoyment and achievement: The pupils' voice. Listening to the voice of *Every Child Matters. Education 3–13,* 36 (4): 393–401.

Hopkins, E. (2010) Classroom conditions for effective learning: Hearing the voice of Key Stage 3 pupils. *Improving Schools,* 13 (1): 39–53.

Kent, P. (2012) The case for using student voice in selection and recruitment: Reflections from a school leader. *Management in Education,* 26 (3): 148–149.

Kher, N., Molstad, S. and Donohue, R. (1999) Using humor in the college classroom to enhance teaching effectiveness in 'dread courses'. *College Student Journal,* 33 (3): 400-406.

Korobkin, D. (1988) Humor in the classroom: Considerations and strategies. *College Teaching,* 36: 154–158.

Lundy, L. (2007) 'Voice' is not enough: Conceptualising Article 12 of the United Nations Convention on the Rights of the Child. *British Educational Research Journal,* 33 (6): 927–942.

Ofsted (2011) *Schools and Parents.* Available at www.gov.uk/government/uploads/systems/uploads/attachment_data/file/413696/Schools_and_parents.pdf (accessed 3 September 2016).

Ofsted (2015) *The Common Inspection Framework: Education, Skills and Early Years.* Available at www.gov.uk/government/uploads/system/uploads/attachment_data/file/461767/The_common_inspection_framework_education_skills_and_early_years.pdf (accessed 3 September 2016).

Peart, S. (2013) *Making Education Work – How Black Boys and Men Navigate the Further Education Sector.* London: Trentham/Institute of Education Press.

Rajeeb, D. (2009) Pupil views? No, let them make decisions. *The Times Educational Supplement,* Issue 4850: 23.

Thomson, P. (2008) Children and young people: Voices in visual research. In P. Thomson (ed.) *Doing Visual Research with Children and Young People*. London: Routledge.

United Nations (1989) *The United Nations Convention on the Rights of the Child*. London: UNICEF.

University of Ulster (n.d.) *Communication Skills: Making Practice-Based Learning Work*. Ulster: University of Ulster, Available at http://cw.routledge.com/textbooks/9780415537902/data/learning/11_Communication%20Skills.pdf (accessed 20 October 2016).

Weinrauch, J. D. and Swanda J. R. (1975) Examining the significance of listening: An exploratory study of contemporary management. *International Journal of Business,* 13 (1): 25–32.

Whitty, G. and Wisby, E. (2007) *Real Decision Making? School Councils in Action*. DCSF-RB001 Research Brief 311. Available at http://webarchive.nationalarchives.gov.uk/20130401151715/http://www.education,gov.uk/publications/eOrderingDownload/DCSF-RB001.pdf (accessed 23 October 2016).

Woods, P. (1976) Having a laugh. In M. Hammersley and P. Woods (eds) *The Process of Schooling: A Sociological Reader*. London: Open University.

Wyness, M. (2009) Children representing children – participation and the problem of diversity in UK youth councils. *Childhood,* 16 (4): 535–552.

8 Preparation and development for leadership

Relevance to practice

Chapter aims

When you have finished reading this chapter you will be able to:

1. recognise the kinds of leaders we want to have in our schools;
2. identify what leadership qualities and behaviours are needed in managing some complexities in education;
3. understand how we prepare and develop such leaders of the future;
4. show how leadership development activities benefit schools at different levels.

Overview of chapter

Experienced and aspiring/middle leaders of the future need to know that tomorrow will not be the same as today. This means they need to develop a greater critical understanding of three issues: the complex challenges educationalists face, how they can resolve these issues and how they lead and manage others to resolve issues. Aspiring/middle leaders are those who are heads of department in secondary settings or key stage coordinators in primary settings who want to further their career. At the start of this chapter we argue that leading and managing complex issues in multi-faceted educational settings requires effective leaders. We therefore consider the leadership qualities and behaviours that are required for such challenging times. We then look at what leadership preparation and development is needed to lead organisations of different sizes and shapes for the future. We define organisation in this chapter as a school, college, academy or children's services, which will be known as settings. We end the chapter by showing how leadership development activities benefit settings at different levels.

> **Key words:** aspiring/middle leaders; educational complexity; leadership preparation and development; succession planning.

Introduction

Schools in England vary in size and shape ranging from academies to community, foundation and faith schools. This adds a different set of challenges requiring different types of leadership (Lumby and Coleman, 2016: 3). This has led to reflection on the nature of the preparation and development required to encourage good leadership. In the twenty-first century, the role of the leader is becoming complex, requiring specific preparation. We are noticing paradigm shifts including the expansion of the role of the principal setting's leadership, the increasing complexity of school contexts, and managing the diversity of the learner population brought about by recent global events in migration patterns. So we have to recognise that leadership preparation is a moral obligation and acknowledge that effective preparation and development make a difference (Bush et al., 2006). We are seeing headteachers getting older – whereas in 1977 headteachers retired aged 40-plus, a decade later in 2007 they are retiring at 50-plus (Todman et al., 2009; Hill, 2009). So where are the future aspiring/middle leaders to be recruited from? We need to grow our own leaders by spotting talent early on and by continuing to build and embed skills, abilities and good practice.

Future leaders will need to continue to manage variations in and across schools to achieve high standards for all (OECD, 2009). According to Munby (2011), schools are not working together as much to deliver continuing professional development because of their own school's day-to-day pressures. Hence, this requires strong leadership qualities to develop action based on resilience, determination and help from others (Munby, 2011). The success of our education system depends on addressing these variations and having world-class leaders in this sector. Future aspiring/middle leaders need to be ready for this challenge and opportunity.

What kinds of leaders do we want in our schools?

We want leaders who are effective at influencing and supporting teachers to promote high-quality learning (Leithwood et al., 2006). According to the National College (2012), effective leaders focus on teaching, learning and people to ensure the current and future success of schools. Today, schools are encouraged to grow their own leaders through in-house staff development as well as spotting and building talent through nurturing, coaching and mentoring and giving staff whole-school challenges to lead and manage. These strategies are tried and tested and have borne dividends according to some international studies in Singapore and South Korea (Goh, 1997; Moorosi and Bush, 2011; Hairon and Dimmock, 2012). We need a national strategy for leadership to deliver school improvement with support from governing bodies to make the right appointments and make the process fit for purpose.

In looking at what kind of leaders we wish to have in our future schools, we draw on Leithwood et al.'s (2006) research, which identified 'seven strong claims' about successful school leadership. These have been expanded to 'ten strong claims' by Day et al. (2010). A potential model of a future leader could include these dimensions:

1. Build vision and set directions;
2. Understand, develop and motivate people;
3. Redesign the organisation;
4. Manage the teaching and learning programme;
5. Know how to use the idea of distributing leadership.

(Adapted from Leithwood et al., 2006)

It appears, according to the National College for Leadership of Schools and Children's Services (NCLSC) (2011: 7), that future leaders will need to be creative and have skills of collaboration, as in working in academies or in securing resources in multi-agency teams to support learners in settings. They will need business planning skills to marshal resources and make best use of professional expertise. They will need to continue to be confident and courageous to challenge orthodox solutions and come up with new ones.

Challenges for leaders

Before describing these qualities and behaviours, we need to discuss the consequences of ageing leadership, recruitment and retention. There is literature (Todman et al., 2009; Munby, 2011), which suggests that existing leaders in settings are getting older, thereby necessitating looking for new leadership from existing aspiring/middle leaders or recruiting externally. Both need strategic planning. Another trend being noticed is that experienced leaders are leaving the profession prematurely, causing a recruitment issue. The reasons for early retirement are complex and include increased workload and complexity of the leadership role (Woods et al., 2012). With the loss of experienced leaders, succession planning becomes quite a challenge. Initiatives like 'fast-track' programmes for 'middle management' and 'grow their own' leaders (Bush et al., 2009; Brundrett and Rhodes, 2010) are the few initiatives in England that have energised leadership development, but there still remains a paucity of applications to leadership, especially in the secondary sector of education (Brundrett and Rhodes, 2010). Those who stay in education require greater support to help them further plan for realistic scale and pace change.

Munby (2011) describes other challenges. They are: achieving high standards for all; leading and managing highly autonomous settings (England has the second most devolved system in the world, second only to the Netherlands [OECD, 2010]); high accountability; and increasingly diverse settings (with approximately 21,000 schools in England, including academies, faith schools, free schools, grammar schools and comprehensive schools). Each of these four challenges are discussed next.

Achieving high standards for all. Future leaders will continue to be proactive in encouraging staff to ensure their practice is the best and they are doing everything possible to achieve high standards. For example, in one middle-sized primary school, key stage coordinators worked together to model transformative leadership to deliver the school's vision for effective teaching and learning that promoted high achievement for all.

Leading and managing highly autonomous settings. England has the second most devolved system in the world, second only to the Netherlands (OECD, 2009). The growth of academies in the last 18 months will enhance this characteristic. For example, in a large multi-ethnic urban school, the heads of departments (as aspiring/middle leaders) took responsibility to deliver a creative curriculum based on developing learners' skills as 'learners as researchers'. So the school was able to deliver the National Curriculum in an innovative manner as they were supported by senior leadership and governors to take risks.

High accountability. All settings in England are accountable to many stakeholders for how they are providing education for their learners. In one special school, the key stage coordinators developed a user-friendly newsletter for parents to show what the school was doing over the academic year.

Increasingly diverse settings. There are approximately 21,000 schools in England, including academies, faith schools, free schools, grammar schools and comprehensive schools. Such increased diversity forms a barrier for future leaders that prevents schools from sharing practice and expertise (Munby, 2011).

Let us turn next to describing how future leaders resolve complex issues and what preparation and development will be required.

Resourceful leader: Common problems, different solutions

As the earlier discussion about the four 'big' challenges school leadership is facing suggests, our current problem is not a conventional one, so it will require unconventional solutions on how we can prepare and train current and aspiring leaders (Bush et al., 2009). Here, Coleman's (2011) notion of a resourceful leader might be helpful to explain. A resourceful leader informs and shapes practice by learning from and using others (National College, 2010) and, as such, exhibit some key characteristics or behaviours. The eight core behaviours of a resourceful aspiring leader are shown in Figure 8.1.

These eight behaviours support and build on the leadership qualities framework (National College, 2010).

Six aspiring/middle leaders in an urban multi-cultural school in the Midlands undertook the 'Leading from the Middle' course (National College for Leadership of Schools, 2006), aimed at developing their leadership skills by focusing on personal areas for development.

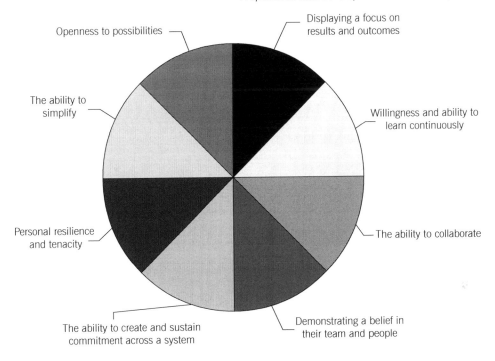

Figure 8.1 Characteristics of a resourceful leader (after Coleman, 2011)

They were coached by the writer of this chapter and interviewed to collect evidence of their growth and development on the programme. Coleman's resourceful leader model (Example 8.1) was used to analyse the findings.

Case study 8.1: Experiences of aspiring/middle leaders in a multi-cultural secondary school

All the knowledge, skills and attributes shown in the following tables are adapted from National College (2011).

Core behaviour 1: Openness to possibilities

Steve, the head of English described openness to possibilities as 'being open to new ways of working to resolve problems before they arise'. Steve knew the faculty members very well and, by being open-minded, led change in the faculty with ease because he created the environment where the team was 'thinking creatively and differently' (McKimm and Phillips, 2010: 145). The range of knowledge, skills and attributes that are required for each of the eight behaviours are noted in subsequent tables.

Table 8.1 Core behaviour 1: Openness to possibilities

1. Openness to possibilities		
Knowledge	*Skills*	*Attributes*
Knowledge of local needs and practices	Partnership working	Openness
Knowledge of effective systems and practices	Team building and working	Adaptability and flexibility
Knowing what resources are needed and available	Relationship building and management	Pragmatism
		Positivity

Core behaviour 2: The ability to collaborate

Leading collaboratively for Jamshaid, head of Maths, meant: 'I am working closely with my team members to develop a consistent approach to teaching of evidence-based problem solving in the faculty.'

Table 8.2 Core behaviour 2: The ability to collaborate

2. Behaviour: Leading collaboratively		
Knowledge	*Skills*	*Attributes*
Knowing what resources are needed and available	Partnership working	
Understanding how to access and utilise knowledge from the frontline	Team building and working	Shared values and purpose
	Relationship building and management	Adaptability and flexibility
	Strategic thinking	

Core behaviour 3: Demonstrating a belief in their team and people

Demonstrating a belief in their team and people meant for Joy, head of Humanities, that 'we are a small team who get results from working closely with my team, doing whatever it takes and often working outside normal school hours'. Thus Joy demonstrated a culture of trust (McKimm and Phillips, 2010) where staff felt valued and motivated (Stoll, 2009).

Asha is the key stage coordinator for Maths in a small primary school. She wanted to try out the 'Singaporean' approach to teaching Maths as it achieved high outcomes for learners. Asha had a good collaborative partnership with two other primary schools who were keen to be involved in this initiative to further improve their learners' attainment in Maths. So regular termly meetings of staff occurred, staff visited each other's schools to observe, share ideas and work with the Singaporean teachers who had come over to England for two weeks. This example shows that Asha believed in trying out new things, sharing good practice and being open to new ways of learning.

Table 8.3 Core behaviour 3: Demonstrating a belief in their team and people

3. Behaviour: Demonstrating a belief in their team and people		
Knowledge	*Skills*	*Attributes*
Knowledge of different personality types / communication styles	Team building and working	Commitment
Due process and employment law	Relationship building and management	Shared values and purpose
		Supportiveness

We will look at a few examples next from children's services where the author facilitated a programme for developing aspiring/middle leaders.

Core behaviour 4: Personal resilience and tenacity

Personal resilience and tenacity is required in leaders but also needs building in the people they serve, with a children's centre coordinator commenting: 'it is so important to develop resilience within families and build their social capacity'.

Table 8.4 Core behaviour 4: Personal resilience and tenacity

4. Behaviour: Personal resilience and tenacity		
Knowledge	*Skills*	*Attributes*
Knowing who to ask for support	Data analysis and monitoring	Tenacity and rigour
Knowing when and how best to fight your corner	Seeing the bigger picture	Adaptability and flexibility
		Pragmatism
		Positivity

A comment from an education, training and employment coordinator about creating and sustaining commitment across a system said that it requires 'leading by example and to work closely to solve problems ... Doing it alone is no longer an option as the problems at times are too big, so we need a different pair of eyes'. This coordinator was addressing the issue of the high levels of NEETs (young people not in education, employment or training) teenage pregnancy. Through successfully involving partners, and believing and supporting young people, she found there had been a 32 per cent reduction in the teenage pregnancy rate. NEETs have also been significantly reduced.

Table 8.5 Core behaviour 5: Create and sustain commitment across a system

5. Behaviour: Create and sustain commitment across a system		
Knowledge	Skills	Attributes
Understanding ways to motivate others for incentivisation	Relationship building and management	Commitment
Knowledge of effective systems	Strategic thinking	Shared values and purpose
		Modelling

One example where a participant felt that they had the ability to create and sustain commitment across a system was where they had been able to lead and articulate a vision for change to a range of people, including elected governors, and secure sustained commitment. Others described examples where they changed the way they communicated with staff and achieved better working relationships as a result.

Core behaviour 6: Focusing on results and outcomes

Focusing on results and outcomes, according to McKimm and Phillips (2010), is often a slow and fragmented progress. One aspiring deputy head of commissioning reported: 'In developing our pilot project, trying out a new policy of endless chances, I used ideas around moral consensus, urgency and equity, and this brought together the right people, to focus on our outcomes.'

Table 8.6 Core behaviour 6: Focusing on results and outcomes

6. Behaviour: Focusing on results and outcomes		
Knowledge	Skills	Attributes
Knowledge of effective performance management systems and workforce development practices	Data analysis and monitoring	Tenacity
Understanding how to access and utilise knowledge from the frontline	Ability to learn from the frontline	Rigour
	Seeing the bigger picture	Commitment
		Pragmatism

Core behaviour 7: Ability to simplify

An advice and guidance worker within a youth justice setting said of the ability to simplify: 'it's easier to communicate when the field of interest is the same'. Grint (2010) argues that leaders need followers to build a sense of community with a common interest and language. This is done by developing a common understanding and consensus among people of the vision for their activity and in their context.

Table 8.7 Core behaviour 7: Ability to simplify

7. Behaviour: Ability to simplify		
Knowledge	*Skills*	*Attributes*
Knowledge of effective systems and practices	Strategic thinking	Adaptability and flexibility
	Relationship building and management	Pragmatism
	Communication	Positivity
	Presentation	
	Seeing others' points of view	

Core behaviour 8: Learning continuously

Learning continuously for a deputy head of youth work involves: 'Doing whatever it takes means listening and learning from wherever and whoever.'

Table 8.8 Core behaviour 8: Learning continuously

8. Behaviour: Learning continuously		
Knowledge	*Skills*	*Attributes*
Knowledge of effective performance management systems and workforce development practices and utilise knowledge from the frontline	Partnership working	Adaptability and flexibility
Understanding how to access	Team building and working	Openness
Knowing what resources are needed and available	Relationship building and management	Commitment
Knowledge of local needs and practices	Strategic thinking	
Knowledge of effective systems and practices	Data analysis evaluation	

This section has explored the eight core behaviours of resourceful leaders in children's services in one area of England, and the underpinning knowledge, skills and attributes required for resourceful leadership. 'The most highly effective leaders of children's services consistently display a common set of eight behaviours in their leadership practice, which collectively is best described as resourceful' (Coleman, 2011, PowerPoint presentation, slide 5).

Understand how we prepare and develop such leaders of the future

We build our argument on two key points: first, leadership is a dedicated profession that requires particular preparation which is different to teacher preparation, and second, without a greater focus on effective preparation and development, we are unlikely to succeed at building world-class education systems. 'School leadership is second only to classroom teaching as an influence on pupil learning' (Leithwood et al., 2006: 12). Furthermore, Ofsted (2010/11) have noted that, 'Given the importance of leadership and management in securing school improvement, there is an urgent need to build more capacity among school leaders' (Ofsted, 2010/11: 4).

An earlier section of this chapter explored in detail the necessary skills and behaviours of a resourceful leader. These attributes will help leaders to be prepared for the complex tasks of leading and manage settings. We develop ideas next of what is effective in preparing and developing aspiring/middle leaders.

General principles of leadership preparation and development

Leadership preparation and development in any context and culture is seen as an important moral obligation (Bush, 2008: 113). This means that leaders are entitled to specialised preparation in order to be effective leaders. We see that there is a difference between leadership *preparation* and leadership *development*. Leadership preparation enhances the skills, knowledge and understanding of the tasks, roles and responsibilities of being a leader, whereas leadership development involves developing knowledge that promotes understanding to improve practice (Armstrong, 2009), thereby having an element of personal learning. In the context of education, this means that staff need to be well prepared and developed for their role so that they can utilise their skills in understanding how organisations actually function to promote high-quality education for their students.

Different approaches to leadership preparation and development

There are various models, but we believe they need to be based on the following principles advanced by Burgoyne et al. (2004), namely:

- knowing that... (focused on effective communication);
- knowing how... (focused on entrepreneurial skills);
- behaviour change... (focused on outward thinking);
- changes to attitudes/feelings... (focused on attitudes/feelings).

In our view, such process-rich learning appears to be better than the content-heavy approach reported by Glatter (2008). What is not desirable is 'identikit' approaches to the preparation and development of current aspiring/middle leaders. Approaches to development of aspiring/middle leaders requires setting up goals like the ones shown below (Simkins et al., 2006):

1. Having a clear understanding of supply and demand for leaders.
2. Taking steps to actively retain talented leaders.
3. Offering shared training and development by working with other settings.
4. Sharing insight, expertise and learning – within and outside the setting.
5. Accelerating the development of people with significant potential for senior roles.
6. Creating a common leadership culture and talent pool.
7. Deepening existing collaborative bonds.

Central to any form of personal development is understanding how adults learn and Mezirow's (2000) transformational adult learning theory emphasises the need to look at how we know rather than what we know, and the importance of developing trusting relationships (Baumgartner, 2001). What appears to make a difference to leadership preparation and development at any level is support from credible peers, through mentoring and coaching; opportunity to access and observe excellent practice; time for reflection; access to high-quality research; and opportunities to discuss with peers and to work with them on common issues (National College, 2011). But this is dependent on time, money and other priorities in the setting.

How do we grow aspiring/middle leaders?

A study by the National College for Leadership of Schools and Children's Services (2010: 119–120) lists a number of approaches:

*   role models – perceptions, talking and walking;
*   experience – bursaries, projects, shadowing, placements, job swaps, enquiry visits;
*   personal support – having the conversations, coaching and mentoring, peer networks;
*   a systematic approach to identifying talent and not wasting talent;
*   personalised, blended learning programmes;
*   school partnership models to grow new leaders;
*   building capacity through practice.

The Hay Group (2007) suggested job shadowing to observe and work closely with more senior leaders, and job rotation where people work in unfamiliar functions or contexts.

Case study 8.2: Columbus School and College, Essex: Senior leader development through mentoring and coaching

(Adapted from National College, 2010: 10)

Columbus School and College is a federation of two special schools which serves 3–19-year-old pupils and students. There is a strong commitment from chief executive Malcolm Reeve to developing its two most senior leaders. The two sites enable both to exercise campus management roles, with each managing one of the two sites in turn for certain periods of the week. Future planned rotation of their respective roles, following a period shadowing each other, will enable these two leaders to gain the range of skills, knowledge and understanding to lead their own schools. Both have progressed from being teachers at the schools to their current positions and have recently gained the National Professional Qualification for Headship (NPQH).

Development opportunities for both so far have included:

1. Leadership coaching by an external business coach following an initial online profiling diagnostic. The diagnostic helped to identify their leadership

predispositions, strengths and development areas. Coaching has been face to face or over the phone.

2. Working alongside an achievement advisor from a consultancy who offers a range of support, including one-to-one on-the-job training. The consultant offers both senior leaders advice, such as personnel management techniques, that can be applied as issues arise during the day. Techniques are tried by the senior leader and their impact discussed in a feedback session: 'It is the bit that's personal, that's what makes the difference,' senior leader 1 says.

3. Regular meetings with the chief executive who provides coaching and mentorship linked to their areas of leadership activity and offers guidance on dealing with management issues.

4. The chief executive's observation of key leadership activities, for example a meeting with parents and verbal feedback on the strengths and weaknesses of how they handled it.

Case study 8.3: Aspiring/middle leader development

Mark is an assistant head responsible for professional development in a large inner-city secondary school. His task was to provide and lead a personalised leadership programme within the school for aspiring/middle leaders. Mark used a number of approaches using coaching techniques such as forming a learning set, reflection activities, working with peers individually and in teams, enhancing their problem-solving skills and developing their role as a leader and manager. This was based on developing high levels of trust based on honesty and openness.

Q Discussion: Case studies 8.2 and 8.3

Both case studies demonstrate the commitment of the headteachers to develop their staff. The key focus of their strategic thinking and planning was school improvement and how it should be led. Different approaches required careful analysis of individual needs to assess the best cost-effective programme for each. Decisions about leadership development were linked to the needs of the school. Aspiring/middle leaders were identified and recruited on the basis that they could help meet these needs. Where the headteacher was not directly involved in preparing the aspiring/middle leaders, they had delegated the responsibility to experienced staff. Observation, feedback and an improvement agenda all guided the development process of the aspiring/middle leaders. Each school developed its own approach to developing leaders, thus showing that preparation and development is context-based and unique to each setting.

How leadership development activities can benefit schools at different levels

It is suggested that any preparation and development opportunities given to aspiring/middle leaders have benefits at three levels, based on personal experience as a staff development leader in a multi-cultural school in the Midlands.

Individual

Individuals report increased confidence and self-belief. Their awareness of the role of aspiring/middle leaders and the skills needed to fulfil these roles were heightened. Their leadership and management skills improved, particularly in relation to managing people. They are now keener to aspire to a leadership role in future and, in a number of cases, their careers have progressed.

School

Staff felt that an investment was being made in their development, which reinforced their commitment to the school and so helped the school to retain them. Staff motivation levels rose and the capacity of the school increased. These aspiring/middle leaders were focused on school improvement which had a direct influence on the quality of provision and learner outcomes including achievement. Leaders were also better able to contribute to strategic thinking. It also gave these leaders a sense of personal investment in the development of staff who they line-managed or supported. The development of leaders gave positive messages to others relating to expectations and opportunity, fostering a new culture of aspiration.

Whole school working together

The pool of leadership talent available within a local area and further afield was expanded. Collaboration sent out the message that schools were working together for each other's good and promotions to leadership roles had been developed through opportunities offered by everyone in the 'system' to model system leadership.

Finally, how do we know that the suggestions for preparation and development of aspiring/middle leaders have an impact on practice? Kirkpatrick and Kirkpatrick (2006) propose five levels of impact of development:

1. **Reach:** how many people take part in the development opportunities.
2. **Engagement:** participants' evaluation of the development opportunity, captured through feedback forms at the end of the session.
3. **Learning:** how much new knowledge and insight participants gain from the development captured through assessments, tests and interviews.
4. **Application:** whether participants act differently in their daily role as a result of the development, captured through observation and feedback.
5. **Impact:** contribution to improved organisational outcomes as a result of the development captured through performance management procedures.

Summary

This chapter gave an overview of how schools are changing, requiring new styles of leadership based on effective leadership qualities and behaviours to manage complex educational environments. There is no 'one-size fits-all' preparation and development programme or 'identikit' for aspiring/middle leaders. Each setting is unique, requiring unique approaches with strategic succession planning developed from local needs. We have argued that holistic development of leaders will make a difference to the learners, learning and the staff themselves. So leadership development activities benefit schools at different levels.

References

Armstrong, M. (2009) *Armstrong's Handbook of Management and Leadership*, 2nd edn. London: Kogan Page.

Baumgartner, L. (2001) An update on transformational learning. In S. Merriman (ed.) *The New Update on Adult Learning Theory*. San Francisco, CA: Jossey-Bass.

Brundrett, M. and Rhodes, C. (2010) *Leadership for Quality and Accountability in Education*. London: Routledge.

Burgoyne, J., Hirsh, W. and Williams, S. (2004) *The Development of Management and Leadership Capability and its Contribution to Performance: The Evidence, the Prospects and the Research Need*. Department for Education and Skills and Lancaster University.

Bush, T. (2008) *Leadership and Management Development in Education*. London: Sage.

Bush, T., Glover, D. and Sood, K. (2006) Black and minority ethnic leaders in England: A portrait. *School Leadership and Management,* 26 (3): 289–305.

Bush, T., Briggs, A. R. J. and Middlewood, D. (2009) The impact of school leadership development: Evidence from the 'New Visions' programme for early headship. *Journal of In-Service Education,* 32 (2): 185–200.

Coleman, A. (for National College) (2011) Resourceful leadership: How directors of children's services lead to improve outcomes for children. Presentation to Belmas Conference, Wyboston Lakes near Cambridge, 2011.

Day, C., Sammons, P., Hopkins, D., Harris, A., Leithwood, K., Gu, Q. and Brown, E. (2010) *Ten Strong Claims about Successful School Leadership*. Nottingham: National College.

Glatter, R. (2008) *A Brief Synthesis of Selected Reports and Documents on Leadership Development.* Nottingham: National College of School Leadership.

Goh, C. T. (1997) *Shaping Our Future: Thinking Schools, Learning Nation*. Singapore Government Press Release. Speech by Prime Minister Goh Chok Tong at the opening of the 7th International Conference on Thinking, 2 June. https://www.moe.gov.sg/media/speeches/1997/020697.htm (accessed 2 February 2016).

Grint, K. (2010) The cuckoo clock syndrome: Addicted to command, allergic to leadership. *European Management Journal*, 28: 306–313.

Hairon, S. and Dimmock, C. (2012) Singapore schools and professional learning communities: Teacher professional development and school leadership in an Asian hierarchical system. *Educational Review,* 64 (4): 405–424.

Hay Group (2007) *Rush to the Top: Accelerating the Development of Leaders in Public Services.* Available at www.haygroup.co.uk (accessed 10 November 2016).

Hill, R. (2009) *The Importance of Teaching and the Role of System Leadership: A Commentary on the Illuminas Research for the National College.* Nottingham: NCSL.

Kirkpatrick, D. and Kirkpatrick, J. (2006) *Evaluating Training Programmes*, San Francisco, CA: Berrett-Koehler Publishers.

Leithwood, K., Harris, A. and Hopkins, D. (2006) Seven strong claims about successful school leadership. *Journal of School Leadership* & *Management*, 28 (1): 27–42.

Lumby, J. and Coleman, M. (2016) *Leading for Equality – Making Schools Fairer*. London: Sage.

McKimm, J. and Phillips, K. (eds) (2010) *Leadership and Management in Integrated Services*. Exeter: Learning Matters.

Mezirow, J. (2000) *Learning as Transformation: Critical Perspectives on a Theory in Progress*. San Francisco, CA: Jossey-Bass.

Moorosi, P. and Bush, T. (2011) School leadership development in Commonwealth countries: Learning across the boundaries. *International Studies in Educational Administration*, 39 (3), ISSN 1324-1702.

Munby, S. (2011) Keynote speech at the 2011 Annual Seizing Success Conference. Available at: www.nationalcollege.org.uk/index/events/conference2011/conference2011-videos/conference2011- videos-munby.htm (accessed 3 November 2016).

National College (2010) *The National Succession Planning Framework for Children's Services.* Nottingham: National College. http://www.virtualstaffcollege.co.uk/index.php/succession-planning-for-childrens-services/dcs-succession-planning/ (accessed March 2012).

National College (2011) *School Business Director Programme Participant Handbook: Pilot Programme*. Nottingham: National College.

National College (2012) Leadership of a self-improving system. Keynote speak by S. Munby, Chief Executive of National College, to headteachers, 5 January 2012, NC.

National College for Leadership of Schools (2006) *Leading from the Middle*. Nottingham: NCSL.

National College for Leadership of Schools and Children's Services (NCLSC) (2010) *Leadership Succession: A Framework for Action for Dioceses and Other Providers of Schools with a Religious Character.* www.leadership-succession-a-framework-for-action-for-dioceses-and-other-providers-of-schools-with-a-religious-character.pdf (accessed November 2016).

National College for Leadership of Schools and Children's Services (NCLSC) (2011) *Identify and Grow Your Own Leaders.* www.nationalcollege.org.uk/index/leadershiplibrary/leadingschools/leading-an-effectiveorganisation/successionplanning/identifying-developing-talent/growing-your-own-leaders.htm (accessed 5 November 2016).

OECD (2009) *International Migration and the United Kingdom: Report of the United Kingdom SOPEMI Correspondent to the OECD*. http://polaris.geog.ucl.ac.uk/research/mobility-identity-and-security/migration-research-unit/pdfs/Sop09_Final_ONSCmnts_SE.pdf (accessed 6 March 2012).

OECD (2010) *International Migration and the United Kingdom: Report of the United Kingdom SOPEMI Correspondent to the OECD*. http://www.geog.ucl.ac.uk/research/research-centres/migration-research-unit/pdfs/Sop10_final_2112.pdf (accessed 6 March 2012).

Ofsted (2010/11) *The Annual Report of Her Majesty's Chief Inspector of Education, Children's Services and Skills 2010/11*. https://www.gov.uk/government/uploads/system/uploads/attachment_data/file/379294/Ofsted_20Annual_20Report_2010-11_20-_20full.pdf (accessed 20 November 2016).

Simkins, T., Coldwell, M., Caillau, I., Finlayson, H. and Moran, A. (2006) Coaching as an in school leadership development strategy: Experiences from Leading from the Middle Journal of In-Service Education, 32 (3): 321–340.

Stoll, L. (2009) Capacity building for school improvement or creating capacity for learning? A changing landscape. *Journal of Educational Change*, 10 (2/3): 115–127.

Todman, P., Harris, J., Carter, J. and McCamphill, J. (2009) *Better Together: Exploratory Case Studies of Formal Collaborations between Small Rural Primary Schools*. London: Department for Children, Schools and Families.

Woods, C., Armstrong, P. and Pearson D. (2012) Facilitating primary head teacher succession in England: The role of the school business manager. *School Leadership and Management*, 32 (2), April 2012: 141–157.

9   Global dimensions and emerging ethical issues

Chapter aims

When you have finished this chapter you will be able to:

1. explain what is meant by the term globalisation and how this is linked to primary education;
2. understand how globalisation can be embedded in primary schools;
3. identify how practitioners and leaders can promote learner awareness of globalisation through pedagogical practice.

Overview of chapter

This chapter presents a conceptual framework for understanding the term globalisation and how it links to primary education. Globalisation is then explored as a concept to see how relevant knowledge is generated using ideas from empirical and methodological studies. We use reflections on critical race theories to shed light on to the contested nature of race/ethnicity and its links to globalisation. The role of leaders is reviewed in embedding globalisation ideas into the primary curriculum, be they thematic or subject orientated. We look at what support strategies might be useful for globally diverse learners such as those with English as an Additional Language (EAL). The notion of partnerships with the wider community is considered to further develop a critical review of the curriculum showing a global perspective. Finally, with the rise of Islamophobia noted in different press, this is a timely moment to reflect on what the ethical issues are and what leaders can do to address some of these in an educational context.

Key words: globalisation; leadership; primary education.

Introduction

In the twenty-first century, many countries have experienced growth in both the economy and population. Through education, we have the opportunity to debate what the impact of this growth means in the context of primary education to help learners understand issues of a global nature. Learners are very perceptive and aware of issues in the world from an early age and it is important to start in the primary school when learners are forming ideas, making friends with different ethnicities and forging connections between the world and education.

Consequently, collectively we can develop a greater understanding and awareness among leaders and practitioners of pedagogical and ethical arguments of a globalised curriculum to move to help eradicate 'poverty and inequalities' (Kosogorin and Barker, 2015: 27) and 'address race inequities in schools' (Flint and Peart, 2015: 5). Globalisation is an ongoing process that can connect people, places and countries through foods, fashions, music and trends from around the world. But it can also cause tensions through a lack of understanding regarding differences and inequality. Globalisation as a concept has started to have a profound impact on people, their culture, their environment and their lifestyles in different ways, perhaps through greater interconnectivity brought about by living in a 'globalised age' (Bottery, 2008: 2). As a result, we all now need to understand the impact of globalisation on ourselves.

With the current issues of migration, especially in Europe, the 'injustice and inequalities in society' (Learning and Teaching Scotland, 2011: 8) require us to realise that our lives are intertwined with others and therefore dependent on others around the world. Within a primary educational context, globalisation describes how a school has a global vision to support the learning of learners so issues such as 'climate change and global poverty' (ibid.) are addressed by future generations in innovative and ethical ways. The advancement of technology and the internet has enabled schools to become more creative in the delivery of the curriculum for their learners and has helped open up the world outside of the immediate classroom and school environment. This has implications for school leaders to critically reflect on their organisation's ethos, pedagogy, staffing and links with the community to help promote a more global perspective. This chapter begins with understanding what globalisation is and its associated layers and how this can be linked to education. Next, it considers critical race theory and the impact of this on school leaders. The discussion then focuses on how primary school leaders embed globalisation through meeting the needs of global learners such as those with English as an Additional Language. Finally, some ethical issues associated with globalisation are highlighted before discussing strategies for moving forward.

What is globalisation?

In the widest sense, globalisation can be defined as 'the world wide diffusion of practices, expansion of relations across continents, organisation of social life on a global scale, and the growth of a shared global consciousness' (Ritzer, 2004: 160). Bottery suggests that this global consciousness is another way of looking at 'global culture' (2008: 5). Therefore, in the simplest terms, globalisation can be seen to be the integration between countries to aid the growth of the global economy in a multitude of ways. Simply put, globalisation is about a common process that brings nations together to share economic, political, social, religious and cultural ideas that can be brought about through advances in communications, technologies, transportation and infrastructure. It also offers opportunities and challenges to see how education can bring about a greater awareness of each other's cultures, languages, customs and rituals through debate and dialogue. This opens minds and hearts through global reach, and develops a shared global consciousness described by Ritzer (2004).

Globalisation has benefits as well as challenges. One key benefit of globalisation is the increased speed and ability of communications which help support a greater knowledge and understanding of global situations. This has helped to increase the rate of change and development and competition. A negative aspect of wider access to technology as a result of globalisation could include shorter working timescales leading to greater pressure to achieve targets.

 Activity: A global curriculum

1. Consider what may be some positive and negative aspects of developing a global curriculum in your setting.
2. How could some of these challenges be overcome?
3. Identify what aspects of globalisation are already taking place in your setting.

 Discussion: Aspects of globalisation

Globalisation is not an external part of the curriculum, rather it should be considered central to the curriculum in ways such as the expansion of ICT – welcome to McWorld. It is about sustainable development and, as educators, our role is to provide opportunities and experiences to learners to support this. Rikowski (2002) suggests that there are four key dimensions of globalisation (which we have simplified and adapted) through the model shown in Figure 9.1.

The first dimension is the outer layer, which is about the idea of the big society where there is likelihood of cross-fertilisation of different members of society. This maximises the chances of the mixing of cultures, leading to increasing hybridity such as cross-cultural marriages producing a mix of values, ideals and beliefs. The second dimension is the middle layer which focuses on the trends, developments and

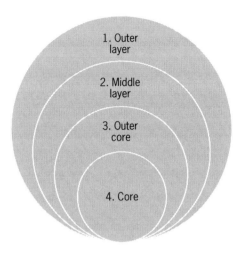

Figure 9.1 Layers of globalisation

characteristics that have resulted from globalisation, for example, through fashion, music and food trends from around the world. The third dimension is the outer core which is linked to the way in which people live in a given context, such as people who live in a specific location and have to co-habit. The fourth dimension is the core which looks at labour and the impact of this on the labour force. For example, in the core element schools offer an opportunity to utilise the skills and experiences of their staff to bring in a more holistic way of working, adding a global dimension to their teaching and learning. Where there is an insufficient knowledge base, the suggestion is to look at reaching out to the local and wider community for such enrichment.

How does globalisation link to education?

Although there has been scant literature on the link between globalisation and primary education (Mistry and Sood, 2012), the impact of globalisation has presented us with 'new opportunities and challenges' which require 'a different approach to education' (Learning and Teaching Scotland, 2011: 8). It is important for all learners to gain the 'knowledge, skills, values, and attitudes to adapt and thrive' (ibid.), and educators have a key role to play in enabling all learners to be prepared to 'live and work in a global society' (ibid.). Emphasising education is a powerful tool to open minds and hearts through rethinking and restructuring education to help learners become global citizens. Education must help prepare the new generation to question racist, sexist inequities and structures and systems that bring about oppression (Gillborn, 2009: 55–58). A primary curriculum informed by equity and fairness from a globalised curriculum offers opportunities to strive for a just society and ethical educational practice remains a crucial process to move towards greater justice.

Education provides learners with a better 'chance of employment … better lifestyle, power, and status' (Chinnammai, 2005: 1). According to Chinnammai (2005: 1), 'education is undergoing constant changes under the effect of globalisation', implying greater inter-connectivity and sharing through the power of the internet. One example of this heightened inter-connectivity is 'twinning' where one school in a developed country is paired up with another school in a developing country. Inter-school communication is promoted via e-links to share examples of school practice and compare similarities and differences. This 'knowledge transfer' (Chinnammai, 2005: 1) between developed and developing countries is a direct result of globalisation in education and aims to help improve learners' knowledge and understanding in both countries. Nations coming together promotes lowering of boundaries and gives learners in classrooms greater access to parts of the world they would not normally connect with.

Leaders in schools need to consider how globalisation can be promoted through role play cross-curricular links within the National Curriculum. There are a variety of ways in which globalisation is embedded in daily practice such as the use of images in visual learning to assumptions about learner's home life and culture. One example in an Early Years setting is the role-play area which can be arranged like a family home where learners have the opportunity to cook foods and dress up in different clothes – which can then be used as a stimulus for discussion and writing. Changing trends in fashion, foods and music can be seen as good opportunities to embrace difference brought about through globalisation and mixing. Teaching and discussions through a global curriculum can facilitate greater open-mindedness and critical consciousness among staff and learners in a balanced pedagogical dialogue.

? Reflective questions

1. In what ways have you developed global awareness in the primary classroom?
2. Can you give any examples of this?

Chinnammai (2005) discusses how globalisation can be better understood from a sociological perspective which emphasises how globalisation can influence learners as individuals within their society and culture. For example, if learners have been able to work with people from diverse cultures then they will have a greater awareness of the different cultural practices between them. However, as leaders and practitioners, we cannot assume that this is always the case and therefore productive leaders will find ways to embed cross-cultural learning into the curriculum as explained by Case study 9.1.

Case study 9.1: Embedding cross-cultural learning

Tina was a Key Stage 2 teacher in a large village primary school in a rural part of the Midlands in England. She had been in the same school for ten years and decided to broaden her experience by changing schools. Tina moved to a more urban school which provided greater responsibilities as part of her new management role. In her new job she was responsible for leading whole-school curriculum development. This new school also had a higher proportion of diverse learners in comparison to Tina's old school which had just a few isolated learners with EAL.

Part of Tina's role was to ensure that a global perspective was embedded into the curriculum to ensure that all learners had the best possible learning experiences. Tina was unsure of what was meant by global perspectives so she began by looking for links associated with celebrations and festivals associated with the pupil population. These links were then embedded into various topics. However, the term 'global perspective' still caused her confusion. With advice from the headteacher, Tina was given time during a training day to see ways in which other staff embedded global perspectives in their planning through their themes. What she realised is that staff had different interpretations of the terms 'globalisation' and 'global perspectives' and were therefore doing different activities in different year groups. For example, many activities were done through play in the Early Years to demonstrate differences between learners, their foods, their clothes. In Key Stage 1, more focus was given to festivals and celebrations, whereas in Key Stage 2 more emphasis was given to cultural issues. It was evident all staff were carrying out age-appropriate activities, but it was unclear how these all linked together to ensure progression and how staff learning was shared across the whole-school team.

Q Discussion: Case study 9.1

Case study 9.1 demonstrates how there can be different understandings of globalisation in an educational context. While there was ample evidence to show globalisation being captured through the Early Years Foundation Stage (EYFS) and the National Curriculum (NC), the exercise demonstrated a need for a more holistic approach to embed globalisation. Schools can do this through firstly having a whole staff discussion on what globalisation means to them within the context of their pupil population, then moving onto the activities they do through their curriculum to promote this. Next, the suggestion is that schools need to ensure that progression in activities that promote globalisation is evident so that pupil knowledge and understanding is progressive to help them become more global citizens in the future.

This is by understanding how things change in the world and having a chance to discuss the impact of these changes. In this way, learners may have a better understanding of different people, and be more resilient to change.

---

⑦ Reflective questions

1. Look at ways in which each key stage can embed globalisation into the curriculum and then share these ideas as a whole school.
2. Identify at least three examples of how talking about globalisation has improved pupil knowledge and understanding of the world – for example through assemblies and follow-up classroom work.

Global education is about providing opportunities to explore issues locally, nationally and internationally. This sharing of knowledge about different cultures, beliefs and values will affect how learners learn and develop. It is also about ensuring learners learn about fairness, equality, justice and human rights through dialogue and debate about real issues happening around the world as a means of developing their critical consciousness. Embracing local and wider community knowledge will enhance the teaching and learning of the next generation of learners.

Critical race theory

Critical race theory (CRT) deconstructs racial inequality in society. Developed in America, CRT is underpinned by a belief that race is a significant form of social oppression (Delgado and Stefanic, 2001). Furthermore, CRT tries to understand the social context of people or a group of people by being aware of how they 'organise themselves along racial lines and hierarchies, and also how they try to better themselves' (ibid., 2001: 2). Originally, in the 1970s, CRT combined two main areas; 'critical legal studies and radical feminism' (ibid.: 2). The legal aspect was an understanding that not every legal outcome was just because individuals will decode facts in different ways according to their perspective, upbringing and outlook. Radical feminism helped to develop CRT through the construction of 'social roles … patterns and habits' which then informed individuals' and groups' thinking and actions (ibid.: 2). CRT proclaims racism as a fact which privileges white supremacy. However, 'race and races are (also) a product of social thoughts and relations' (ibid.: 3). For example, on a domestic level two neighbours of different race and colour may form good social relations based on personal experiences and may be able to ignore societal preconceptions. However, two other neighbours of different race and colour may be highly influenced by societal structuring and, as a result of race, will hold a deep hostile suspicion of one another. Although CRT originated from the law field, it can be applied to many other areas such as education to explain aspects of equality and equity for all learners in schools.

⟨?⟩ Reflective questions

1. How can you teach about the principle of CRT in your classroom?
2. What strategies will you use for your different learners?
3. What strategies will you choose for culturally diverse and/or culturally similar learners?

Through case studies and individualised examples of 'being neighbourly', one can find out more about each other's interest, hobbies and likes and dislikes, thus leading to forging good relationships. Exchanging communications with partner schools where the culture and language is different to UK-based learners may seem daunting initially, but opens doors for inter-connectivity and forming longer-term relationships.

In education, CRT can be used to explore classroom dynamics between learners and to ascertain whether race has an impact on learners' daily interactions. CRT may offer us a tool to help us dismantle discrimination and structures of oppression. Flint and Peart (2015) argue that we need to arm ourselves with the language that helps us to conceptualise what the vision of an ethically globalised curriculum looks like so that we can support practitioners and learners to critically argue against oppression that disempowers and disenfranchises some sections of society.

Impact of critical race theory on school leaders

School leaders need to be aware of CRT and its potential impact in classrooms when engaging with differences in race, culture and beliefs. Even very young learners will begin to recognise differences in skin and hair colour between themselves, especially through their conversations in play. One strategy about how conversations about differences can be addressed is through the topic of ourselves (a key early primary school topic), whereby learners are actively encouraged to look at themselves and compare themselves with their peers. These differences can then be celebrated to make each pupil feel unique, rather than being isolated or excluded. Other topics in primary school such as my family, or people around me, also help to focus on diverse cultures so that differences in food, customs and dress can be shared and better understood. Religious Education is another forum which can help learners better understand others' beliefs, thus helping each of us to become better informed and more open-minded. However, as leaders, we need to be careful that misconceptions are not taught inadvertently. For example, not everyone from any given cultural group will have similar religious beliefs. In contemporary society the increase in cross-cultural marriages now means traditional religious beliefs are interpreted in different ways to suit current lifestyles, as illustrated by Case study 9.2.

Case study 9.2: Cultural differences

Melisa was a seven-year-old girl in a primary school. Her father was a white British Christian, while her mother was of Indian origin with some Hindu beliefs. Both parents spoke to Melisa in English, which was their home language, however key festivals on both sides of the family were celebrated to ensure that Melisa had developed an understanding of both cultures. The family tried to attend church most Sundays as they felt it was important for Melisa to have an understanding of faith and belief. However, after a while Melisa's father started a new job which involved more time away from home. Consequently, family visits to the church on a Sunday declined as Melisa's mother felt uncomfortable attending church without her husband.

Q Discussion: Case study 9.2

Case study 9.2 shows that with mixed marriages on the increase, parents still want the best for their child. Most parents try very hard to make sure that their child has the best of both sets of parents in terms of their cultural background and heritage, but with working patterns changing this is not always easy. For primary school teachers this means that communication with parents in different ways to be aware of the family culture and background is even more important, especially if parents do not pick their children up from school due to other responsibilities.

Reflective question

From your personal knowledge of your learners' ethnicity, languages and cultures, what opportunities do you offer to embrace diversity in your setting to demonstrate a global population?

In a more globalised world, we can learn from each other through discussions, debate and other classroom activities to start to empathise and develop a deeper understanding of differences compared to the majority of peers in the group.

How primary leaders embed globalisation

Globalisation has an impact in shaping learners' learning experiences at all levels in education. Leaders need to be aware of practitioner values and beliefs and the ways globalisation in the curriculum is permeated through individual practitioner and pupil behaviours. For example, a practitioner from a bilingual and multi-religious background may have a wider understanding of certain customs and traditions of their pupil population in comparison to a practitioner who is monolingual and of no religious orientation. Leaders need to consider how opportunities to embed globalisation through the primary curriculum are practised, making the best use of the staff skill set.

In the Early Years this may include offering as many opportunities through play and active learning as possible, with relevant supporting learning aids such as puppets, toys, pictures and video clips. In lower primary it may include using resources such as books and the internet to allow learners to ask questions to enhance their understanding, or making links with schools in different parts of the world via the internet so that learners have the opportunity to ask one another about their lives. For upper primary learners it will include using the British Government's Prevent Strategy (DfE, 2011) to ensure that they have a safe forum to discuss contemporary issues highlighted in the media and social network sites to help inform learners' decision making. As educators we need to be careful that we are not always telling learners what to do – but rather providing them with the tools and information for them to make an informed and just choice.

As a result of globalisation, many aspects of the primary curriculum have changed. The integrated use of technology and social media to connect with different learners around the world can support learning. Learners in schools need to be taught the possible consequences of unsafe internet practices. The right conditions must be established for safe use of technology across the school, which will enable learners to use technology for learning. Case study 9.3 considers how this positive learning culture might be established.

Case study 9.3: A positive learning culture

Molly was a leader in a primary school. In addition to being a class teacher for learners aged eight to nine, her main responsibility was to lead Geography and Literacy across the whole school. The day after 9/11, most of the learners in her class came into school talking about what they had seen on TV. Some of her learners had been in awe of how planes could be used to demolish buildings. However, one girl in her class was very upset as she was supposed to be going on holiday to Spain and now was too scared to travel. Molly tried to start the day off in her class in the normal way by introducing the Literacy session, but she soon realised that the learners were off-task and the conversation repeatedly returned to events they had seen on the TV and what their parents' opinions of the situation had been.

Molly decided to stop the session and took a different perspective. She asked the learners to describe exactly what they had seen on TV and to discuss the event, and the consequences of this incident, with a partner. The ensuing discussion was purposeful and focused as all the learners wanted to talk about it. As the week progressed, the learners were given many opportunities to ask questions about those who lost their lives and discuss ideas in groups.

Q Discussion: Case study 9.3

Case study 9.3 shows the global impact of one horrific incident which reverberated around the world, impacting all our lives. By adapting her planning for the week, Molly responded to pupil interest and needs, which took learning in a different direction in a safe and secure manner.

Reflective questions

1. How has the curriculum been adapted in your school to help learners deal with global issues highlighted in the media?
2. What is the impact of providing these opportunities for learners to better understand what is happening in the world beyond the classroom?

Support for learners with English as an Additional Language (EAL) and globalisation

As a result of increasing migration, the pupil population of England is rapidly changing, and meeting the needs of learners with English as an Additional Language (EAL) is becoming more paramount. These learners are coming from all over the world, therefore gone are the days when learners in a setting tended to come from only one or two parts of the world. Nowadays, learners are coming from many different countries, with languages that are unfamiliar to us, therefore this section focuses on how some of the needs of learners with EAL are met through globalisation being addressed in the curriculum. To support learners with EAL, practitioners should talk to the class about the origins of all pupils, especially if they are a new arrival from abroad, and show the class on a map where the country is located. In that way the mind map of learners is extended in terms of extending geographical knowledge and understanding. Practitioners should share with the class if learners with EAL speak multiple languages and what these languages are so as to

Table 9.1 Strategies to support global learners such as those with EAL

Examples of a global approach in the primary curriculum (Early Years, Key Stage 1 and Key Stage 2)	Strategies to support learners with EAL
Inclusion – use of a range of topic-based resources (artefacts, books, photographs, vocabulary labels for items) (from the Early Years and KS1 National Curriculum)	Try to put some of these resources on a table-top display to allow learners to see and feel them. Allow learners to use these resources as a stimulation for collaborative conversations and writing
Inclusion – being involved (from the Early Years, EYFS and National Curriculum)	Pair learners to have responsibility in the classroom to encourage cooperation and communication
Reading (from the Early Years and KS1 National Curriculum)	Use ICT to have read-aloud texts to support learners' correct use of language and contextual understanding
Topic – 'Ourselves' (from the Early Years curriculum)	Look at specific differences such as skin, hair and eye colour and celebrate these. Challenge learners' understanding of what white, black, brown really mean
Topic – 'My family' (from the Early Years and KS1 curriculum)	Identify different members in a family (who has extended family living with them?) and share this information as a class through photographs
Topic – 'Healthy eating' (from the Early Years and National Curriculum)	Look at the different foods eaten by the learners in the class outside of the school environment and reflect on any differences and where the food comes from. Identify different foods eaten by EAL learners and offer opportunities for the rest of the class to experience these, such as different fruits or desserts
Topic – 'Cultural celebrations' (from the Early Years and National Curriculum)	Identify the different festivals associated with the pupil population, and understand the reason for celebration. Make learners who celebrate different festivals other than Christmas feel special too

promote a deeper understanding of each other. In terms of globalisation, Table 9.1 shows how leaders can support practitioners to help learners with EAL (for a more detailed discussion see Mistry and Sood, 2015).

Table 9.1 begins with general classroom strategies for supporting learners with EAL through both the Early Years and National Curriculum before moving onto some specific primary topic-based strategies. One suggestion to involve learners with EAL more in class input for topics is through 'show and tell', paired talk or group activities, where home experiences and traditions can be shared and valued. It is important to note that Table 9.1 only focuses on one part of globalisation, which is to support learners with EAL. There are a number of other ways in which school leaders can devise a more global approach as suggested by the list below:

- Allow parents to contribute to the curriculum with any ideas they have to support topics in school, which in turn can be a discreet way of building partnerships.
- Encourage learners to share differences in customs, traditions and rituals, regardless of faith or religion, in a sensitive manner.

- Clarify what British values means to the pupil population through connections in learning.
- Make the curriculum flexible so that current issues in the media can be discussed to help facilitate better understanding.
- Encourage learners to share their opinions on issues and be able to give reasons for these opinions, but also be clear on the consequences of their opinions.

It is important to remember that incidents around the world, such as the Charlie Hebdo attacks in Paris in 2015 or bombing in Belgium in 2016, should not fuel a blame culture between the learners in the class. Leaders need to support practitioners in offering a local and global perspective so that learners understand that although atrocities do happen in the world, it is not individuals' responsibility. Crucially, it is about addressing global issues through other areas of learning such as Citizenship or Personal Social and Emotional Development so that learners learn about personal responsibility and are able to make rational decisions. Finally, every opportunity to build positive relationships with all parents should be taken to help support the work of the school.

 Activity: Strategy

Activity: Working towards a more global approach

Using the relevant curriculum (Early Years and National Curriculum), devise a table similar to Table 9.1 (which shows common topics in the primary curriculum) to show a more globalised approach for your setting through the topics that are covered.

Ethical issues associated with globalisation

As globalisation refers to the greater inter-connectivity between people and places, it also implies greater dependency on different nations for certain goods and services. With this greater dependence comes a range of ethical issues which need to be addressed to ensure fair working practices. With greater global influences on our thinking and daily lives, educational leaders and practitioners working in diverse settings have a professional ethical responsibility to:

- understand government policy relating to extremism, radicalisation and terrorism;
- implement government policy on counter-terrorism;
- help to identify local issues and threats;
- work with school-based colleagues and other relevant agencies to monitor activity and report any issues to the appropriate authorities.

(Peart, 2015)

The DfE has defined extremism as 'vocal or active opposition to fundamental British values including democracy, the rule of law, individual liberty and mutual respect of different faiths and belief', and radicalisation as 'the process by which people come to support terrorism and extremism and, in some cases, to then participate in terrorist groups' (DfE, 2011: 7). Extremism to radicalisation is a journey, it does not happen instantly although there may be pivotal events which can support (and possibly accelerate) this progression. However, before radicalisation can occur, the external context (ideology, organisation, circulation mechanism) and internal disposition (vulnerability, susceptibility, motivation/potential) need to be present (Peart, 2015). We are advancing an argument about this issue here as we have a fundamental duty of care to our learners and we need to understand what the implications of extremism ideology might be for the citizens of the future. An ideology forms the bedrock of extremism and radicalisation and is the set of core beliefs which drives the movement. The ideology does not have to be wholly consistent, but there must be sufficient agreement to produce a degree of coherence.

Peart (2015) suggests that in a global context, vulnerability is about whether individuals can identify commonality with the mainstream society. It is about whether they feel they fit in and belong to a given society. In terms of susceptibility, it is about whether individuals are easily influenced by others or not. Essentially it is about picking up on clues which indicate if individuals are impressed by certain actions or behaviours, or if they are seeking a different kind of lifestyle. The motivation or potential is if extremism and radicalisation appear to offer answers to difficult questions or whether extremism helps some individuals make sense of the world. Furthermore, it is realising if radicalisation provides a context where individuals feel at home.

There are many diverse ideologies that can lead to extremism and radicalisation. Such ideologies are often based on a blame culture which seeks to accentuate difference. Globally, there have been significant changes in the nature of extremism in recent times as illustrated by Case study 9.4

Case study 9.4: An awareness of extremism

James was a Year 6 teacher in a primary school with a 60 per cent EAL pupil population. Part of the staff meeting in the school one week focused on being aware of conversations and any signs that may suggest learners were aware of any aspect of extremism and radicalisation. Although James had not discussed these specific terms with his class, he was aware they had emerged during the week as his class was working on writing newspaper articles as part of their Literacy sessions based on current media issues. Part of the homework set that week was based on reading selected newspaper articles to become familiar with various arguments.

However, during playground duty James overheard a conversation between a group of Year 6 learners discussing the bravery of girls who left the UK to live in Syria as jihadi brides. James was shocked that these quiet, polite, able Year 6 learners had an awareness of issues in Syria. He spoke to his headteacher as soon as his playground duty was over and they decided that this conversation between the learners needed to be the focus for the staff briefing the following morning for all school staff and also for the senior leadership team meeting later on during the week. The decision was made that all staff needed to be aware of learners' conversations regarding any controversial issues to assess whether these conversations needed further clarification, or whether they were just an expression of interest.

Q Discussion: Case study 9.4

The lesson learned in Case study 9.4 was that all school staff need to be vigilant as to the kinds of conversations taking place between learners, both in class during activities but also outside the class, around the school, to ensure that issues are dealt with sooner rather than later.

Reflective questions

1. Could you imagine these situations happening in your educational setting?
2. How well prepared would you feel if one of the current headlines involved one of your learners in some way?
3. What actions does the school need to take now to respond?
4. What systems/procedures does the school need to develop or put in place?

Impact on practice: Way forward

The government has emphasised the importance of promoting fundamental British values in the English primary curriculum which can support globalisation in a positive way through learners being 'encouraged to regard people of all faiths, races and cultures with respect and tolerance' (DfE, 2014: 4). In practice, this means all school staff need to make sure that learners 'understand that while different people may hold different views about what is right and wrong, all people living in England are subject to its law' (ibid.) and leaders need to monitor this and also to ensure that learners are 'made aware of the difference between the law of the land and religious law' (ibid.). Promoting these fundamental British values is intended to help school staff maintain high standards of behaviour and ethics practice among pupils. Examples of activities that leaders can promote in schools might include:

- work on the strengths, advantages and disadvantages of democracy and how democracy and the law works in Britain, in contrast to other forms of government in other countries to give a more global perspective;
- giving all learners within the school a voice that is listened to in tandem with practical demonstrations on how democracy works by actively promoting processes such as a school council whose members are voted for by the learners;
- using opportunities such as general or local elections to hold mock elections to promote fundamental British values and provide learners with the opportunity to learn how to argue and defend points of view;
- providing teaching resources from a wide variety of sources to help learners understand a range of faiths around the world;
- extra-curricular activities, including any run directly by learners, in promoting fundamental British values.

(DfE, 2014: 6)

In reference to globalisation the suggestions from the DfE (2014) imply that all learners need to feel valued and respected from an early age through the inter-connectivity of the curriculum with supporting ICT. If learners have the opportunity in the primary sector to ask questions about global issues, then they will have the foundations for a more global understanding. Furthermore, leaders need to promote diversity and inclusion for all future citizens.

Summary

Essentially globalisation is about how we as human beings act within the world, and how in turn the world affects us. In our dynamic world, one effect of globalisation on education has been the opportunity to explore new contexts and cultures of different people through technology which has promoted 'global values for global citizenship' (Mistry and Sood, 2012: 2). However, while there are many benefits of globalisation, leaders need to be continually alert to potentially damaging influences of globalisation such as extremism and associated extremist organisations, which may influence learners' future behaviour.

> ### ☞ Reflective questions
>
> 1. What more could you do to embed globalisation in your school?
> 2. What ethical issues for learners are emerging in your school as a result of globalisation?
> 3. How are leaders supporting the management of these ethical issues to have an impact on practice for pupil learning?

References

Bottery, M. (2008) How different are we? Globalisations and the perceptions of leadership challenges in England and Hong Kong. *Journal of the British Education Studies Association*, 1 (1): 1–16.

Chinnammai, S. (2005) Effects of globalisation on education and culture. ICDE International Conference, 19–23 November 2005, New Delhi.

Delgado, R. and Stefanic, J. (2001) *Critical Race Theory: An Introduction*. New York: New York University Press.

Department for Education (DfE) (2011) *Prevent Strategy*. London: DfE.

Department for Education (DfE) (2014) *Promoting Fundamental British Values as Part of SMSC in Schools: Departmental Advice for Maintained Schools*. London: DfE.

Flint, K. and Peart, S. (2015) Is there any justice in being other than 'white' in Britain? *Race Equality Teaching*, 33 (2): 5–9.

Gillborn, D. (2009) Risk-free racism: Whiteness and so-called 'free speech'. *Wake Forest Law Review*, 44 (2): 535–555.

Kosogorin, A. and Barker, L. (2015) Global learning in primary education: Moving beyond charity. *Race Equality Teaching*, 33 (2): 27–32.

Learning and Teaching Scotland (2011) *Developing Global Citizens within Curriculum for Excellence*. Scotland: Teaching and Learning Scotland.

Mistry, M. and Sood, K. (2012) How are leaders integrating the ideology of globalisation in primary school contexts? *Education 3–13: International Journal of Primary, Elementary and Early Years Education*. IFirst Article (1–13).

Mistry, M. and Sood, K. (2015) *English as an Additional Language in the Early Years: Linking Theory to Practice*. London: David Fulton.

Peart, S. (2015) *Extremism and Radicalisation – Whose Responsibility?* Nottingham: Nottingham Trent University.

Rikowski, G. (2002) *Globalisation and Education*. A paper prepared for the House of Lords Select Committee on Economic Affairs, Inquiry into the Global Economy, 22 January 2002.

Ritzer, G. (2004) *The Globalization of Nothing*. London: Sage.

10 The changing role of leaders in Early Years education

Chapter aims

When you have finished reading this chapter you will be able to:

1. understand the role of a leader within Early Years;
2. be aware of the changing role of leaders in the context of Early Years;
3. develop your understanding of some of the challenges faced by these Early Years leaders;
4. have a range of strategies to help support your development and practice.

Overview of chapter

The role of leaders is multi-faceted and ever changing, dependent on learners, curriculum, policy and individual contexts. Leaders in Early Years settings can have the greatest influence on the way in which learning is tailored and personalised for the benefit of young learners. This chapter will begin by firstly looking at the different types of Early Years settings and the leaders within them. Secondly, it will critically reflect on what the role of an Early Years leader is and how this role has changed within the Early Years age phase. Leading any kind of diverse workforce (such as nursery nurses, teaching assistants, key workers, teachers and specialist staff) is a challenge within its own right. However, within Early Years a unique set of challenges is presented and considered next, due to the nature of the age phase, the variety of settings and the different and more creative ways in which learning and teaching take place through the Early Years Foundation Stage (EYFS) (DfE, 2014). Finally, it will highlight some of the challenges faced by leaders along with strategies for moving forward, before concluding what constitutes effective leadership in Early Years.

Key words: Early Years; leadership; pedagogy.

Introduction

The quality of learning and teaching in Early Years is influenced by the quality of staff and their understanding of what constitutes excellent Early Years practice. According to Coughlin and Baird (2013: 1), there has been greater emphasis on the 'importance of leadership in Early Years'. This implies that the Early Years phase is now recognised as an important phase of the education system in England. The White Paper, *Educational Excellence Everywhere* (DfE, 2016), also emphasises the importance of excellent leaders and teachers in settings to help raise the quality of education for all learners, which includes the very early stages of education such as Early Years. The role of leaders in all aspects of education is complex because of the range of responsibilities they have, such as being accountable for raising standards to improve outcomes for all learners, leading and managing staff learning and professional development, and safeguarding within changing climates and central policy. In addition, specific to Early Years are the vital tasks of leading and managing transition and fostering excellent parent–setting partnerships at the beginning of education. One example of this is through Early Years leaders (as well as other Early Years staff) being more visible at the beginning and end of the day so that parents can see them to ask any questions they may have. This visibility and communication is the basis of the foundation for great home–school partnerships. This is seen as common practice in many settings, but maybe primary schools could also try to adopt this approach if possible within Key Stages 1 and 2, to continue to enhance the relationships with parents that have already been developed from the Early Years.

Early Years settings and leadership

Early Years is a unique educational stage. It is perhaps the stage with the greatest variety of settings and leaders in comparison to primary and secondary schools. By this, we mean Early Years settings that are government-registered and have provision for learners aged birth to five years. These include children's centres, playgroups, toddler groups, childminders, nurseries, pre-school groups and foundation stage in schools (Aubrey, 2011). Each of these settings has its own leaders, which can vary from a group/room leader, to a nursery manager to an Early Years leader. Although there are many similarities between all these leadership roles, such as quality of care and education and having a clear vision, there are also specific differences. For example, a nursery manager may also have responsibility for managing the budget for the whole setting as well as the recruitment and retention of staff; in comparison, an Early Years leader in a lower/infant or primary school may not have responsibility for staff recruitment (as this would be the responsibility of the overall leader).

Role of an Early Years leader

The role of a leader in a setting varies from context to context, however, one similarity all leaders have is to lead the setting with a well-planned, clear vision. There are many different types and styles of leadership, however it is well known that in the context of Early Years the majority of leaders are female, therefore masculine traits such as 'aggression, competition and independence' (Blackmore, 1989 cited in Aubrey 2011: 2) may not be as evident in this sector. Aubrey (2011: 27) has identified seven aspects of a leader's role which we feel are important for consideration within Early Years. We have used these seven aspects and adapted them to show you how an Early Years leader can demonstrate their role in practice as shown in Table 10.1.

Table 10.1 Examples of how a leader's role can translate into practice in Early Years

Aspects of a leader's role	*How this can take place within Early Years*	*Specific examples*
Articulate a vision	Sharing the Early Years vision with the Early Years team, the school team, parents and other stakeholders who should support the overall ethos, especially in relation to play-based learning and collaborative activities that promote social awareness of others	Through whole-setting staff meetings then linked to practice through team planning meetings
Quality service	High-quality teaching and learning (DfE, 2016) to ensure learners make progress through indoor and outdoor learning, and also self-initiated independent learning	Having a range of activities that promote challenge and progression in steps
Professional development	Ongoing professional development which is recognised and valued for all staff in the Early Years team, which is cascaded to improve practice for learner impact	Staff being reflective in their practice to identify how improvements can take place and where good practice can be identified
Accountability	Secure knowledge of the different ways in which learners learn, develop and make progress, and to use this knowledge to help with learner assessment	Being confident with the different ways in which assessment can take place to ensure learner progress in different contexts
Collaboration	Working effectively in teams (Belbin, 1993) beyond Early Years in the setting and beyond, and building partnerships with parents and other outside agencies to share good Early Years practice and resources where possible	Being able to work as a team within the setting, where there is respect for roles and responsibilities, and then translating these skills beyond the setting
Responsive to change	Changing practice according to changes in the curriculum (DfE, 2014) and legislation to improve learner outcomes, such as making assessment more integrated with both indoor and outdoor activities so that assessment does not happen in isolation	Being up to date with curriculum and policy changes so that they are embedded positively and part of daily practice
Entrepreneurial approach	Able to take risks to make learning engaging to ensure all learners make progress by having a range of learning experiences both indoors and outdoors and also maximising opportunities for visits in the local community and beyond	Having the confidence to try new strategies to make learning creative and fun, and developing skills of negotiation and business

Table 10.1 shows how aspects of a leader's role can be translated into practice through given examples with the support of the team and other stakeholders. This table also shows that an Early Years leader has a multi-faceted role which is carried out in addition to teaching and other curriculum responsibilities. This can be different to other leaders in a primary or secondary setting whereby some leaders may not have full-time teaching responsibilities.

The role of leaders in Early Years is multi-dimensional in that not only are they leading and managing teaching and learning in a different context (Bloom, 2003), but can also be leading and managing a larger phase team. This is because in the Early Years there is more likelihood of having a team that includes more than the class teacher, and maybe one or two support staff. Staff in an Early Years team may include the teachers, teaching assistants, key workers, nursery nurses, and other specialist staff. In addition, there is the added pressure of ensuring successful parent–school partnerships (a key feature of this age phase), and learner progress in skills, knowledge and attainment. Despite this, Aubrey's research (2011: 27) suggests that the most important aspect of a leader's role is 'to deliver a quality service'. Rodd (2006) suggests that in order to have a quality service, the decision-making process is important. In Early Years, a more collaborative culture is essential in terms of understanding the foundations and theory of how children learn and develop, and using this information through team meetings to support planning and progression. A more diverse team in this sector implies that there can be different levels of knowledge and understanding of child development and how learning should be planned and delivered. This means that decisions based on meeting the needs of learners have to be agreed together as a team (Belbin, 1993) to aid consistency in the setting. One issue with having a diverse staff team could be that the role of leaders in Early Years can be understood in different ways by different members of staff, as illustrated by Case study 10.1.

Case study 10.1: What is my role?

Keya was a reception teacher in her primary school. She was in her second year of teaching with leadership responsibility for the Early Years phase. However, she was unclear as to what the role involved. Keya focused on making certain that Early Years was resourced and that the age phase ran smoothly. She also wrote a new policy for Early Years, but other than that she was confused about what else she needed to do. The primary school was one-form entry so Keya had no other Early Years teachers to compare ideas with from an Early Years perspective. During a staff meeting Keya expressed her concerns as to her lack of understanding as to what the role involved. Her headteacher advised her to make links with other Early Years teachers and leaders in local schools to compare how they led the Early Years phase.

Q **Discussion: Case study 10.1**

Case study 10.1 shows that a collaborative approach to leadership beyond the setting may not be appropriate to support leaders who are isolated in terms of their age phase and subject responsibility. The confusion here is what exactly an Early Years role should be, as leadership varies in different types of Early Years settings. For example, a group leader in a nursery would have a different set of responsibilities to an Early Years teacher in a primary school. By following the advice of her headteacher, Keya made links with two other local schools and then went to each school to see what other Early Years leaders did. She found that she was not alone in some of her worries and was able to work with other staff to share good practice and contribute to her own professional development. The collaboration here was that Keya began to work with others outside of her school environment and then shared these ideas with her support staff. This collaboration gave Keya confidence to lead and manage Early Years more effectively to ensure that her learners made progress.

Reflective questions

1. Reflect on your understanding of how leaders are supported in your setting.
2. Compare this understanding with someone who is in a different setting.
3. Give two examples of the impact of your leadership on learning in your setting (such as planning, teaching or managing staff).

Aubrey (2011: 52) emphasises that the role of Early Years leaders includes 'planning, teaching, coordinating staff, and recording and reporting the progress of pupils'. With all the things leaders have to do, time can be very limited, especially if some Early Years leaders also have additional curriculum or other responsibilities such as being a headteacher or a nursery manager. Furthermore, Ofsted (2013: 7) have said that a major part of an Early Years leader's role is to 'communicate effectively with all and lead by example'. This is crucial for positive relationships to be embedded with learners, parents, other practitioners and outside agencies, to ensure the success of the setting. This is not always easy in an Early Years setting as they are very busy with 'high intensity and pace throughout the day' (ibid.: 52) because of the type of creative and active learning activities that take time to set up on a daily basis. Case study 10.2 illustrates how busy Early Years leaders can be within their context.

Case study 10.2: One Early Years leader's role

Kumari is an Early Years leader in a primary setting. She has been at the setting for five years and has been an Early Years leader for the last two years. In her setting there is a briefing every morning at 8.35 for all staff (including support staff) for daily information. In addition, the leadership team meet once a week at 8 a.m. and once a week after school. Kumari began to notice that her team was always on time (but arrived last) for the staff briefing in the mornings whereas some of the other teams have been in the briefing area for a while, enjoying their morning coffee. Kumari saw that she and her team would always rush to the briefing in the morning after setting up the indoor and outdoor areas, whereas other teams did not have outdoor areas or the same level of creative activities to set up, implying they had more time for other responsibilities. At the end of the day in Early Years, key staff would be visible or be around for parents to talk to before clearing up. This, again, was something that Kumari noticed other leaders not doing, so while she was helping her team clear up or deal with issues with parents, other leaders would be working on their leadership responsibilities.

Q Discussion: Case study 10.2

Case study 10.2 shows that sometimes the nature of learning in Early Years means that time has to be managed creatively, otherwise a leader may not be able to complete their leadership and other setting responsibilities. There is also a need for awareness of the roles and responsibilities of different staff in a setting, as all leadership responsibilities are not on an equal par in terms of the time taken. For example, in a primary school an Early Years leader can be isolated, especially if there is one-form entry meaning that there are very few Early Years staff. In comparison, a manager of a large nursery may not feel the same as Kumari as their working team could be a lot bigger, with more individuals to share the workload. This shows that although all Early Years leaders have very similar responsibilities, the number of staff in a setting can determine the extent of leadership responsibilities.

? Reflective questions

1. What is the role of an Early Years leader in your setting?
2. How does an Early Years leader in your setting manage their time so that teaching and leadership responsibilities are balanced?

The expectations of leaders in any setting change over time. In larger Early Years settings there are more individuals to help out, however, in smaller settings leaders have greater responsibilities which are difficult to divide between the team.

The changing role of Early Years leaders

Early Years has changed over the last ten years. With a revised EYFS (DfE, 2014) curriculum and a more specific Ofsted regime, this sector is becoming more recognised as the foundations of all learning. The changing nature of education in Early Years means that leadership is also changing rapidly to keep pace, as supported by Ofsted (2013: 7) who emphasise that strong Early Years leaders 'make changes possible'. There are several things a leader can do to create more opportunities for change through the planned curriculum. For example, more opportunities for talk could be created by encouraging learners to discuss their ideas with a partner or a group. Thinking time could be encouraged to allow learners time to process and assimilate their ideas, and greater opportunities to share learning could be facilitated either through 'show and tell' or through taking photographs. In a wider sense, it is about how leaders translate government directives and initiatives into practice to ensure that their team do not feel under pressure to go through yet another change. The 2016 White Paper (DfE, 2016) highlights the need for excellent teachers and leaders to help raise standards in education. This has an impact on the way in which settings are led and part of this is making sure that the workforce is well trained. Ofsted (2013: 6) reinforce this message by emphasising that Early Years leaders now need to take responsibility for being 'well qualified and experienced' to ensure that their setting is the best it can be. An example of this is the Early Years Teacher Status (EYTS) qualification which is aimed at raising the status, profile and quality of the Early Years workforce. Even though some leaders in Early Years may not see themselves as leaders in their own right (Mistry and Sood, 2015), this perception is now changing as Early Years is a learning stage in the educational hierarchy with its own leaders. The wider range of staff who work in this sector generate different ways of working which all need to be managed and led effectively. In Early Years the management of relationships tends to be 'both task and person orientated' (Aubrey, 2011: 52). This implies that Early Years leaders have to work effectively with a great variety of people and through people in order to facilitate the transparent working of the setting. Case study 10.3 shows how one leader's perception of what leadership meant in practice changed.

Case study 10.3: One perspective of an Early Years leader

Rohona was an Early Years leader in a large primary school which had three-form entry. She had been an Early Years practitioner for five years before she was given an opportunity to lead the age phase (learners aged three to five). Initially, she thought it would be straightforward to take on the role of Early Years leader, but she soon realised that it was much harder to manage so many different personalities in the age phase. The revised EYFS (DfE, 2014) and the White Paper (DfE, 2016) meant that changes needed to take place to ensure that all staff made even better progress. Leading this change was new as Rohona thought all she had to do was manage the daily running of the setting efficiently. She did not realise that as a leader she would also be responsible for leading staff to lead learning. Her role now involved leading learners, staff and learning, as well as managing budgets and assessments to ensure learner outcomes were raised.

Q Discussion: Case study 10.3

Case study 10.3 shows that good leaders can make leadership look seamless in a setting. Rohana did not realise the extent of what a leader in Early Years did until she had to take over the role. Managing staff in any setting can be tricky, especially if staff have a variety of qualifications and experience. Bringing these strengths together for the benefit of the learners and the setting requires long-term vision with clear manageable steps of progression.

Reflective questions

1. What is your perception of leading in Early Years?
2. How has your perception of leadership changed?
3. Reflect on how you manage your team to be more collaborative in teaching and planning. What does this say about your leadership skills, abilities and competencies?

Change and uncertainty in education is constant. With any kind of change, it is essential for leaders to remember the four key principles of the EYFS (that every child is unique; the importance of positive relationships; learning in well-enabled environments; and for learning and development to take place in different ways) (DfE, 2014) and use these as their foundation for leading learning.

Early Years leadership in practice

The overall leadership structure in many settings is hierarchal, but in the context of Early Years this hierarchy can seem invisible because of a more collegial approach by the team towards getting things done. This section looks at how Early Years leadership is influenced by Ofsted, leading learning and creating an optimal learning environment.

According to Early Years Matters (2016), there are three aspects to leadership within Early Years which consist of: leading others, leading learning, and leading innovation. Leading others includes the immediate and wider Early Years team as well as the learners, parents and other stakeholders. Within this remit of leading others, the emphasis is also on encouraging staff to be critically reflective of their practices to help meet the needs of all learners. Leading learning can only be effective if there is a strong foundation of the philosophy of how learning takes place and how this can be applied in practice for the learners in the setting. It is also about being up to date regarding curriculum and policy changes and trying to make these changes as integrated and seamless as possible. Leading innovation is about accepting that change is normal, it is about taking risks and thinking in different ways such as ensuring that learning is creative and active to make it as inspirational as possible for all.

Ofsted and leadership in Early Years

Wilshaw (cited in Ofsted, 2013: 4) has clarified that the 'importance of Early Years is beyond question'. This reinforces the fact that Early Years is a key phase of learners' education where foundations are set for future learning and life opportunities, and leaders have a key role to play in this process. Ofsted (2013: 6) have emphasised that 'strong effective leadership is the key' to the success of an Early Years setting. This is because one aspect of a leader's role is to raise the quality and standards of a setting, to ensure that pupils reach their highest potential through having a clear vision for the pupils and setting. During their inspections, Ofsted look for a number of features in Early Years:

Inspectors must spend as much time as possible gathering evidence about the quality of teaching and learning by:

- observing the children at play
- talking to the children and practitioners about the activities provided
- observing the interactions between practitioners and children
- gauging children's levels of understanding and their engagement in learning
- talking to practitioners about their assessment of children's knowledge, skills and abilities and how they are extending them
- observing care routines and how they are used to support children's personal development
- evaluating the practitioners' knowledge of the early years curriculum.

(Ofsted, 2015: 14)

The above list is not exhaustive in terms of what Ofsted look for during an inspection, but it is some of the key areas that leaders need to facilitate to ensure that their setting is of high quality.

How do Early Years leaders lead learning in Early Years?

Any learning environment is a space created for learning to take place and, in the context of Early Years, this is both indoors and outdoors (DfE, 2014). Indoor examples include specific zones such as construction, messy play, mark making, reading, number, creative and quiet. The outdoor area can also include similar zones, but in addition they may also be a garden area, a wet area, and larger play apparatus alongside bikes and cars to help learners develop their confidence and gross motor skills. It is important to keep in mind that the learning environment is not just restricted to the setting environment. In the broader sense, this learning environment also includes the home, places of interest, the local area and beyond. All of these areas have an impact on learners' perception and understanding of the world which can be observed through their play. These observations and resulting assessment are crucial in planning the next steps of learning through learners' play.

In creating any kind of learning environment, the role of all adults is vital in supporting the learning that can take place, and the Early Years leader is the catalyst to facilitate this. This means that the Early Years leader needs to be aware of changes such as learners' interests, curriculum changes and the impact of new central initiatives and Acts. The EYFS (DfE, 2014: 3.3) suggests that a 'rich and varied environment' is essential to learners' development in the Early Years. One reason for this is because learners need a variety of stimulating learning to ensure that they are engaged in tasks. If the environment and tasks are not stimulating, then learners may become bored, leading to behavioural issues. This implies that any learning environment created needs to consider aspects of learners' personal, social and emotional development in addition to curriculum development. For example, learners could be working in pairs on identifying number bonds to ten while playing number snap, and during this activity adults would also be looking for learners' social competence, and whether they are able to take turns and share. Another example is if learners are acting out a fairy-tale story with puppets, the adults may also be looking for learners' level of language acquisition and whether they can show any emotion while in role play, as well as whether they have the social skills to work together as a group.

Early Years leaders also need to make sure that they include activities that promote talk and collaboration between learners to help them to become confident and independent in their learning, as discussed earlier. The DCSF (2009: 11) have suggested a number of ways in which learning can take place in any learning environment which we have adapted in Table 10.2 to show you the strategies and skills needed.

Although Table 10.2 is focused specifically on learning within the Early Years, many of these strategies can be used across all sectors of education to meet learners' different learning styles, dependent on the context.

Table 10.2 Examples of how learning can take place in Early Years

How learners learn in Early Years	Our strategies	Suggested skills needed
Playing	• Allowing different opportunities to play both indoors and outdoors whether it is through drama or role play • Encouraging pupils to use resources such as puppets to give them a stimulus in their play	• Creativity • Questioning • Promoting active learning • Utilising indoor and outdoor space • Modelling play by adults
Active learning	• Ensuring that planned activities do not always follow the same pattern – allowing pupils to find things out for themselves • Trying to make learning creative and investigative to encourage independent learning	• Promoting active learning • Utilising indoor and outdoor space • Encouraging investigation and exploration • Questioning
Being with others	• Giving pupils opportunities to work alone, in pairs and as part of a group	• Collaboration • Opportunities to play together • Modelling speech
Using talk	• Allowing the use of talking partners or talking groups to encourage pupils to voice their thoughts • Reflecting on where talk can be used in your planned sessions	• Encouraging collaborative conversations • Using puppets and ICT to encourage talk
Modelling	• Trying to model as much as you can – go into role in play, model correct use of language	• All adults to model • Encouraging confident learners to model, too
Challenge	• Using questioning to challenge pupils further • Encouraging pupils to have a go at finding out something new and sharing it with the rest of the class	• Asking questions • Encouraging learners to ask questions, too
Opportunities for independent learning	• Reflecting on the opportunities for independent learning that are provided beyond reading or sharing books	• Providing time for independent exploration and investigation

Reflective questions

1. Can you give an example of how learners' skills can be promoted in an outdoor learning environment through play?
2. In your setting, reflect on one aspect of the Early Years learning environment that needs to be improved and why.

How Early Years leaders promote pedagogical learning environments

An Early Years leader is crucial in promoting and supporting high-quality learning and teaching environments to ensure that all pupils achieve the best possible outcomes. This means that it is the responsibility of all leaders to ensure that the learning environment created supports the learning of all learners. The EYFS (DfE, 2014) talks about personalising learning as much as possible to ensure that all learners make progress to achieve the best they can. According to Coughlin and Baird (2013: 1) one way leaders can achieve this is through pedagogical leadership which can be defined as the 'guiding of individuals or groups' through having a secure 'understanding of how learning takes place' and the supporting 'philosophy and practice' that supports this process, which is a key aspect of Early Years (Andrews: 2009). In practice, this means that leaders need to be aware of the processes of learning and the way in which people learn, and then use this understanding to lead their team – for example, being aware of the strengths of the team and utilising these strengths to support learners; alternatively, being aware of the weaknesses of the team and ensuring that there is a collaborative approach to help and support team members, with professional development to help them better their practice in Early Years.

This notion of pedagogical leadership seems very fitting within the context of Early Years as leaders in this age phase see themselves as 'partners, facilitators, observers and co-learners' (Coughlin and Baird, 2013: 1). Part of a leader's role is to have the mechanisms in place that support the ethos, values and vision of their organisation. This means that leaders need to support their staff team to articulate these through planning and subsequent

Table 10.3 Examples of creating a pedagogical learning environment in Early Years

Factors	Our suggested strategies
Improve visibility of pupil competencies and contributions	• Display pupil work including interactive table-top displays • Celebrate pupil progress through 'show and tell'
Deepen engagement with partners	• Be available for parents before and after the setting's day and by being visible as much as possible • Have an information board for parents near the Early Years entrance that parents will see as they bring their children through • Make parents feel comfortable to ask questions
Value, promote, celebrate and respect diversity, equity and inclusion	• Celebrate pupil events such as birthdays, special holidays and home events • Share understanding of events that celebrate difference and diversity • Discuss events taking place around the world to allow learners an opportunity to have collaborative conversations
Encourage adults to encourage challenge	• Develop questioning skills in all activities to give learners challenge in their learning
Articulate play and enquiry as learning	• Question learners in play to highlight the learning taking place • Encourage learners to ask each other questions during their learning, too • Share with parents how learning takes place through play
Develop a culture of reflective practice	• Encourage all practitioners and leaders to be critically reflective of their practice so changes can take place for future improvement

activities. For example, if part of a setting ethos is striving for excellence, they may be encouraged to try their best, or to have a go. Leaders should encourage their staff to use meaningful positive praise with learners, and to build up a bank of different ways of praising learners to encourage them to do even better.

One perspective of a pedagogical leader is that they look at how a pedagogical learning environment can be set up and promoted to ensure the highest level of learning possible. Coughlin and Baird (2013: 2) suggest that key factors need to be considered in the creation and promotion of a pedagogical learning environment and these are adapted in Table 10.3.

Table 10.3 shows how key factors can be translated into practice to help support the thinking behind the creation of a pedagogical learning environment.

The challenges of Early Years leadership

Leading and managing pupil learning and staff in any age phase can be challenging. In this chapter you will have read about many challenges faced by Early Years leaders through the text and case studies. As the majority of leaders and practitioners in this sector are female, their ethic of caring may overtake their overview and application of leadership in practice (Gilligan, 1982). However, this caring ethic is essential for all learners to ensure that they feel safe, secure and valued for any kind of learning to take place. One of the main challenges of Early Years leadership is that there is still a lack of leadership training and development (Aubrey, 2011). This is because much leadership training is generic or geared towards education in general, but very little of it is aimed at the contextual nature of Early Years. As a result of this, many Early Years leaders take ownership of their own professional development as a setting or in collaboration with cluster settings. The Early Years sector has a larger variety of staff with varying qualifications (as mentioned earlier), which can be challenging for leaders in comparison to managing a small number of teachers with similar qualifications. In this case, working towards the strengths of the staff and sharing experience is vital to the smooth running of the setting. Another challenge is that many staff in this sector work part time, and therefore managing planning and learning can be difficult, especially if staff do not get paid more than their contracted hours. Here, communication strategies become imperative to ensure that everyone works together as a team.

Strategies for moving forward

Ofsted (2013) have suggested a number of strategies to help leaders in Early Years to move forward with their practice and development. Firstly, leaders need to identify the 'strengths and weaknesses' (Ofsted, 2013: 8) of their setting in terms of their practitioners, practices and policies. This needs to be clear from the outset by having a secure understanding of how young learners learn and develop in order to personalise their learning for the best outcomes. The process of continuous critical reflection is also essential to ensure that the setting as a whole develops over time through reflecting in action and on action (Schön, 1991) individually and as a team. Collaborative learning and sharing good practice is the key here, not only within the actual setting but also between settings to get a wider picture of practices within different contexts. Secondly, 'strong leaders need to seek external challenge' (Ofsted, 2013: 9). This implies that Early Years leaders need to be more pro-active in sharing their vital skills and practice with others to improve Early Years practice. Examples of this include building stronger and long-lasting partnerships with external agencies, including other settings in their cluster area. Thirdly, professional development is highly valued and encouraged by leaders to ensure that the workforce is 'well qualified' (ibid.: 10). This can take place in a number of ways from attending courses to visiting different settings to observe as many different types of practice as possible. Next, all leaders need to 'be accountable' (ibid.: 12) as well as making sure that staff are also accountable for their actions and decisions, too. Finally, all Early Years leaders need to ensure that all practitioners and parents work together as a team so that all are 'involved in pupil learning' (ibid.: 16).

Summary

In this chapter, you have looked at how Early Years has changed and how these changes have had an impact on leaders in the setting. Early Years is a unique phase within an individual's educational journey in England. There are many differences between this age phase and other educational phases that means the role of leader changes at a more rapid pace. Leaders are at the forefront of leading change to ensure that learners have the best possible experience to support learning. In conclusion, learners of the future need education that is fit for the twenty-first century, which suggests that Early Years education has to be liberalising, meaning developing capabilities and the skills of independence, confidence, thinking, risk taking, collaboration and inter-dependency in Early Years classrooms, which set the foundations for young learners to become global citizens.

Reflective questions

1. How has your role as leader changed to support the leading of learning in your setting?
2. As a leader, how can the pedagogical learning environment of your setting be changed to improve pupil learning?

References

Andrews, M. (2009) Managing change and pedagogical leadership. In A. Robins and S. Callan (eds) *Managing Early Years Settings: Supporting and Leading Teams*. London: Sage, pp. 45–64.

Aubrey, C. (2011) *Leading and Managing in the Early Years*. London: Sage.

Belbin, M. (1993) *Team Roles at Work*. London: Butterworth/Heinemann.

Blackmore, J. (1989) Educational leadership: A feminist critique and reconstruction. In J. Smyth (ed.) *Critical Perspectives on Educational Leadership*. London: Falmer Press.

Bloom, P. J. (2003) *Leadership in Action: How Effective Directors Get Things Done*. Lake Forest: New Horizons.

Coughlin, A. and Baird, L. (2013) *Pedagogical Leadership*. Ontario: Queens.

Department for Children Schools and Families (DCSF) (2009) *Learning, Playing and Interacting: Good Practice in the Early Years Foundation Stage*. Nottingham: DCSF.

Department for Education (DfE) (2014) *Statutory Framework for the Early Years Foundation Stage: Setting the Standards for Learning, Development and Care for Children from Birth to Five*. London: DfE.

Department for Education (DfE) (2016) *Educational Excellence Everywhere*. London: DfE.

Early Years Matters (2016) *Leadership*. Available at http://earlyyearsmatters.co.uk/index.php/areas-of-interest/leading-learning/ (accessed August 2016).

Gilligan, C. (1982) *In a Different Voice: Psychological Theory and Women's Development*. Cambridge, MA: Harvard University Press.

Mistry, M. and Sood, K. (2015) *English as an Additional Language in the Early Years: Linking Theory to Practice*. London: Routledge.

Ofsted (2013) *Getting it Right the First Time: Achieving and Maintaining High Quality Early Years Education*. Manchester: Ofsted.

Ofsted (2015) *Early Years Inspection Handbook*. Manchester: Ofsted.

Rodd, J. (2006) *Leadership in Early Childhood*. Buckingham: Open University Press.

Schön, D. (1991) *The Reflective Practitioner*. Aldershot: Ashgate Publishing.

11 Conclusions

Chapter aims

When you have finished reading this chapter you will be able to:

1. understand what are some of the key educational challenges for leaders in English schools;
2. identify some of the implications of change management for leaders;
3. reflect on some ways forward in supporting the development of your practice in the future through our key messages.

Overview of chapter

This book set out to raise awareness of how practitioners and leaders are managing rapid changes in education, and to equip you with knowledge and understanding of some of the wider policy issues and practices deployed in leading and managing change in a variety of educational settings. We are witnessing now more diversity in learning communities in our settings and we have shown you examples of ways in which different settings are using different leadership strategies to manage their own educational challenges. Leadership has changed dramatically with the rise of faith schools, academies and other change directives from the government. In this book we have suggested a range of strategies to lead and manage change successfully to support you rather than take the 'one-model-fits-all' approach. We have used a range of contemporary literature and real-life case studies to illustrate our ideas for you to reflect on. Therefore, this chapter addresses three key areas: firstly, how educational change can pose challenges for leaders; secondly, the implications of change management for leaders; thirdly, some suggested key ways forward for you to consider in your context.

Rapid pace of educational change – a challenge for leadership

Education is dynamic and changes with different central priorities and changing learner populations, but the key is how these changes are led and managed effectively without staff feeling alienated and constantly under pressure of implementing yet another initiative. Changes in legislation such as Ofsted (2010), the SEND Code of Practice (DfE, 2015) and the Equality Act (Equality and Human Rights Commission, 2010) have taken place to accommodate changing times and to improve the quality of education for all groups of learners. Today, all who work in education are responsible for helping to raise standards to help improve learner outcomes. Leaders are also more accountable for supporting their teams to raise standards and improve the quality of learning and teaching at all levels. The educational culture has changed and it has become essential to consider different collaborations and partnerships with other schools and settings beyond the education sector.

We are seeing greater collaboration within and across settings locally, nationally and internationally in an attempt to apply good practice for the benefit of the learners. For example, with greater migration to the UK we are observing the need for schools to be more proactive in meeting varied needs relating to introducing the English language, and cultural and personal identity. We are seeing greater awareness of learners' understanding of events and issues in the world through the media and social media at a younger age, and it is important to allow learners the opportunity to discuss issues of inequality and poverty so that they become active, global citizens. One way this can happen is by understanding and implementing the principles of inclusion and equipping our learners with a voice that challenges stereotypes and discriminatory language and practice.

Implications of change management for leaders

High-quality teaching and learning and high standards of achievement are sought by every leader in education. The White Paper (DfE, 2016) emphasises that leaders need to have a clear vision for improvement, and this vision needs to be promoted as part of a setting's policy of having excellent teachers and leaders to help raise standards. This means that leaders need to be creative, entrepreneurial, moral, ethical and compassionate to support changes and associated challenges. However, we now are facing a lack of talented staff taking up leadership roles as the current leadership sector is either growing older or practitioners are unwillingly forced into leadership positions. We need to grow new leaders with a strong vision to lead in a collaborative manner to ensure that they have the support of their team so that they are not working in isolation.

Key messages of the book

1. All leaders need to work towards excellence of teaching and leadership by providing a full range of opportunities for all learners to help them to become independent and

reflective learners. The curriculum offered in settings has to be fit for purpose in preparing learners to be active, global citizens. This requires the need to provide awareness of what globalisation is and how this is linked to education. We need to work towards embedding a range of strategies to show how globalisation is being addressed through the curriculum. Central to this notion is a need to understand the ethical issues associated with the impact of globalisation, and how some of these can be managed within your context.

2. Schools need good sources of data to plan and provide resources for high-quality education for learners. This requires a good understanding of the policies for inclusion, necessitating all staff to be aware that inclusion is a must and not an added extra. This requires proactive collaboration and partnership with governors and other agents. The rise of academies is one approach seen in the English sector, requiring an understanding of the impact of external and internal drivers that influence policy and practice.

3. With an ever decreasing supply of leaders in the new generation, we need to coach and mentor to foster appropriate levels of confidence and aspiration among new talent to provide high-quality teaching and learning for all learners.

4. Leaders need to be aware of the different issues associated with the recruitment and retention of staff. Specifically, why is there a lack of appetite for leadership roles in some settings, and how can professional development be more focused and personalised to ensure that all staff want to better their practice. Here leaders may wish to consider whether leaders outside the education sector would provide a new way of looking at things.

5. In the climate of constant change, leaders need to be more creative in finding new and different ways of working with new and existing partners to benefit all settings. In one way, this is also about sharing good practice and learning from each other so that we do not become isolated in our setting practice. This collaboration between and beyond settings means that definitions of quality can be explored and shared together for a common understanding to meet the highest possible educational standard for learners.

Ways forward

This section specifically looks at ways in which leaders can move forward in their practice. In the current climate of educational change, leaders in settings need to support the building of partnerships beyond their local area and context in order to share good practice and to learn from each other. As leaders in education we need to be reflective to identify how we listen (daily, weekly or at set times in the term) and act on the voices of stakeholders to not only better our practice, but also to really understand the perspective of others. Furthermore, as leaders we need to think about how our teams are supported in developing these essential skills to help all stakeholders feel respected and valued within busy working schedules. We believe that listening and taking into account user voices means that learners are better supported to help improve their educational outcomes. An innovative leader will always strive for different and more creative solutions based on the strengths of the team to encourage a more collaborative culture. In addition, an innovative leader will think outside the box and not be afraid of taking risks and learning from other settings that are totally different to their own. But, all leaders need the support of their team and the appropriate professional development to help them be confident and competent with the changes in education to help their setting to be successful.

Summary

Educational Excellence Everywhere (DfE, 2016) highlights how aspiring teachers and leaders do make a difference to the quality of teaching and learning for all learners. We have emphasised that tomorrow will not be the same as today so, in summary, what this book suggests is to start from where the energy for change lies, build a coalition within the organisation and seek out pragmatic and entrepreneurial solutions. Leaders need to make sure that the learner is at the heart of the process for any kind of change, and look for what can be influenced rather than controlled. Central to this process is for a leader to be clear about their own and others' values, understanding and working in emotionally intelligent ways and employing an empathetic and encouraging approach. Leaders' moral and ethical obligations are also highlighted as these are the foundations of the individual style of leadership and the way in which leadership development is prioritised and cascaded in a setting. We also hope that such challenges and offer twenty-first-century leaders opportunities to continue to act with greater equality and humanity.

References

Department for Education (DfE) (2015) *Special Educational Needs and Disability Code of Practice: 0 to 25 years. Statutory Guidance for Organisations which Work with and Support Children and Young People who have Special Educational Needs or Disabilities.* Available at www.gov.uk/government/uploads/system/attachment_data/file/398815/SEND_Code_of_Practice_January_2015.pdf (accessed 14 August 2016).

Department for Education (DfE) (2016) *Educational Excellence Everywhere. The School's White Paper 2016.* Available at https://www.gov.uk/government/uploads/system/uploads/attachment_data/file/508447/Educational_Excellence_Everywhere.pdf (accessed September 2016).

Equality and Human Rights Commission (2010) *Equality Act.* Available at https://www.equalityhumanrights.com/en/equality-act/equality-act-2010 (accessed August 2016).

Ofsted (2010) *The Special Educational Needs and Disability Review – A Statement is Not Enough.* Available at www.gov.uk/government/uploads/system/uploads/attachment_data/file/413814/Special_education_needs_and_disability_review.pdf (accessed 13 August 2016).

Index

Introductory Note:
When the text is within a table, the number span is in *italic*.
Eg, carer/parent voices 4, 85–6, 95–7, 96
When the text is within a figure, the number span is in **bold**.
Eg, National College Framework for Leadership 24–6, **25**
Number spans for case studies are underlined, and are also listed under the heading 'case studies'.
Eg, mentoring 27, 92, 94, 105, <u>115–16</u>, 157

Taylor & Francis eBooks

Helping you to choose the right eBooks for your Library

Add Routledge titles to your library's digital collection today. Taylor and Francis ebooks contains over 50,000 titles in the Humanities, Social Sciences, Behavioural Sciences, Built Environment and Law.

Choose from a range of subject packages or create your own!

Benefits for you

» Free MARC records
» COUNTER-compliant usage statistics
» Flexible purchase and pricing options
» All titles DRM-free.

Benefits for your user

» Off-site, anytime access via Athens or referring URL
» Print or copy pages or chapters
» Full content search
» Bookmark, highlight and annotate text
» Access to thousands of pages of quality research at the click of a button.

eCollections – Choose from over 30 subject eCollections, including:

Archaeology	Language Learning
Architecture	Law
Asian Studies	Literature
Business & Management	Media & Communication
Classical Studies	Middle East Studies
Construction	Music
Creative & Media Arts	Philosophy
Criminology & Criminal Justice	Planning
Economics	Politics
Education	Psychology & Mental Health
Energy	Religion
Engineering	Security
English Language & Linguistics	Social Work
Environment & Sustainability	Sociology
Geography	Sport
Health Studies	Theatre & Performance
History	Tourism, Hospitality & Events

For more information, pricing enquiries or to order a free trial, please contact your local sales team:
www.tandfebooks.com/page/sales

 **Routledge**
Taylor & Francis Group

The home of
Routledge books

www.tandfebooks.com